ELIE WIESEL

AN EXTRAORDINARY LIFE AND LEGACY

ELIE WIESEL

AN EXTRAORDINARY LIFE AND LEGACY

EDITED BY
NADINE EPSTEIN

FOREWORD BY
RABBI JONATHAN SACKS

AFTERWORD BY
TED KOPPEL

MOMENTBOOKS
WASHINGTON, DC

MANDEL VILAR PRESS
SIMSBURY, CONNECTICUT

Some of the material in this book originally appeared in Moment Magazine from 1975 to 2018.
Ronald S. Lauder's reflection was originally published in TIME and is used with permission of the author.
Oprah Winfrey's reflection is adapted from her remarks at an Elie Wiesel Foundation for Humanity gala.

This book is typeset in Gotham and Minion Pro. The paper used in this book meets the minimum requirements
of ANSI/NISO Z39.48-1992 (R1997). ∞

Designed by Navid Marvi
Cover photo: Public Domain

Publisher's Cataloging-In-Publication Data
(Prepared by The Donohue Group, Inc.)
Names: Epstein, Nadine, editor. | Sacks, Jonathan, 1948- writer of supplementary textual content. |
 Koppel, Ted, 1940 February 8- writer of supplementary textual content.
Title: Elie Wiesel: an extraordinary life and legacy / edited by Nadine Epstein; foreword by Rabbi
 Jonathan Sacks; afterword by Ted Koppel.
Description: Washington, DC: MomentBooks, [2019] | "Writings, reflections, photographs"—Cover.
Identifiers: ISBN 9781942134572
Subjects: LCSH: Wiesel, Elie, 1928–2016. | Wiesel, Elie, 1928-2016. Nuit—Influence. | Jewish authors—
 20th century—Biography. | Authors, French—20th century—Biography. | Holocaust survivors—
 Influence. | Jews—United States—Identity. | Judaism.
Classification: LCC PQ2683.I32 Z667 2019 | DDC 813/.54—dc23

Printed in the United States of America
15 16 17 18 19 20 21 22 23 / 9 8 7 6 5 4 3 2 1

MomentBooks
Moment Magazine, a division of the Center for Creative Change
4115 Wisconsin Avenue, NW, Suite LL10
Washington, DC 20016
www.momentmag.com/momentbooks
MomentBooks is a trade book imprint partner of Mandel Vilar Press

Mandel Vilar Press
19 Oxford Court, Simsbury, Connecticut 06070
www.americasforconservation.org | www.mvpress.org

Acknowledgments

This volume draws from writings by and interviews with Elie Wiesel that have appeared on the pages of *Moment Magazine* since 1975, and the large body of work, in particular speeches, that he left us when he passed away on July 2, 2016. In addition, Elie's son Elisha and many of Elie's friends, students and colleagues generously shared their time and memories.

A project such as this one is never a solo undertaking. In particular, I thank Marilyn Cooper, Thomas Siurkis, Eileen Lavine and Sarah Breger. Diane Bolz, Sue Driesen, Anna Isaacs, James David Jacobs, George E. Johnson, Ellen Meltzer, Debbie Sann and Ellen Wexler also made important contributions. *Moment* designer Navid Marvi, as always, was an invaluable collaborator.

A dedicated team of *Moment* advisory board members and friends, including Kathryn Gandal, Andrew Mack and Gwen Zuares, helped guide this project to fruition. I am especially grateful for the contributions and guidance of Jean Bloch Rosensaft and Menachem Rosensaft.

This book was funded by *Moment* as well as the Taube Foundation for Jewish Life & Culture, the Albin Family Foundation, Roland Brack, Toby Dershowitz, Terry Grant, Phyllis Greenberger, Sharon Karmazin, Larry and Kathy Kanter, Marcia and Robert Kerchner, Zev Wade Lewis, Andrew and Amy Mack, Philip N. Margolius, Melanie Moreno, Gary Roggin, June and Marvin Rogul, Elizabeth Scheuer and Peter Joseph, Michael Seltz and Gillie Campbell, Robert and Jacqueline Smelkinson and Carol and Robert Summers. Without the support of many friends this book would not have been possible.—*Nadine Epstein*

In memory of
Elie Wiesel
(1928–2016)

Contents

In His Own Words ESSAYS, SPEECHES, INTERVIEWS

About *Night*

Afterword BY TED KOPPEL

Credits

Foreword

BY RABBI JONATHAN SACKS

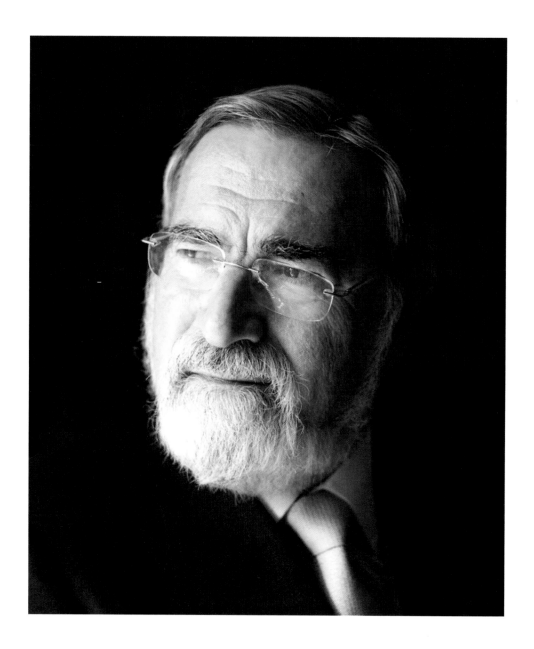

Jonathan Sacks is the former Chief Rabbi of the United Kingdom.
He is the author of more than 25 books, most recently
Not in God's Name: Confronting Religious Violence.

> "Whatever he did and wherever he went, Elie carried with him six million fragments of our people. His was the voice of memory when others sought to forget."

At the end of the book of Genesis, Joseph makes one deeply poignant request. Although he would die in exile, he knew that one day God would bring His people back to their land. When this time would come, he made the people promise that they would: *vehaalitem et atzmotai mizeh*, "Carry my bones with you".

When Moses ascended Mount Sinai, and there was the catastrophe of the Golden Calf, he smashed the tablets and together with God made new ones. Ever afterward, *luchot veshivrei luchot munachim be-aron*, the Israelites carried with them in the Ark the new tablets and the fragments of the old.

It has been this way throughout Jewish history. We carry with us all the fragments of our people's past, the broken lives, the anguished deaths. For we refuse to let their deaths be in vain. They, our past, live on in us as we continue the Jewish journey to the future, to hope and to life.

This has been the case with the victims of the Holocaust, the lost lives, the broken communities, synagogues desecrated and set on fire, the sacred scrolls burned and turned to ash, a million-and-a-half children murdered. What our enemies killed we keep alive in the only way we can, in our minds, our memories and our memorial prayers.

It was this mission, this calling, that defined Elie Wiesel's remarkable life. He was the man who gave voice to the voiceless victims of the Holocaust and bore witness in the name of humanity to one of the great crimes against it.

Whatever he did and wherever he went, Elie carried with him six million fragments of our people. His was the voice of memory when others sought to forget, and of defiant hope in the face of despair. He spoke for an entire murdered generation,

and did so with dignity, humanity and grace. He was a great survivor, a great Jew and a great humanitarian. Elie Wiesel was the man who taught the world to remember what so many wanted to forget. He was the embodiment of the moral conscience of the world.

There are cultures that forget the past, and there are cultures that are held captive by the past. Jews do neither, and Elie showed us how. We carry the past with us as we will carry the memory of the Holocaust with us for as long as the Jewish people exists, as Moses carried the bones of Joseph, and as the Levites carried the fragments of the shattered tablets of stone.

Those fragments of memory help make us who we are. We live for what they died for, when we walk tall as Jews, showing we are not afraid, refusing to be intimidated by the anti-Semitism that has returned to Europe or by the sustained assault on Israel, the one place on earth where Jews have ever been able to defend themselves instead of relying on friends who stayed silent, passive, when our ancestors needed them most.

This book of reflections is a fitting tribute to the legacy of Elie Wiesel. In its pages and through the words of its contributors, you will feel a promise, not just to the souls who perished, but also to Elie and all those who survived Europe's darkest night: we will never forget you, we will not let you down, until Jews can walk the world without fear, witnesses against those who choose death, to the God of life who told us, "Choose life."

Elie's life was one that touched the hearts and minds of the world. In doing so, he was not just a blessing to the Jewish people, but to all of humanity. May his memory be blessed and may we all forever continue to be inspired by his legacy.

Introduction

BY NADINE EPSTEIN

Nadine Epstein is Editor-in-Chief and CEO of Moment Magazine.
She is also a reporter, writer, and the founder of the Daniel Pearl
Investigative Journalism Initiative for young journalists.

"It is critical to keep Elie's memory alive at a time when anti-Semitism and prejudice are again on the rise, and the lessons he taught have been called into question."

Despite our longings, there is no such thing as a super hero. There are only complex human heroes who draw upon their own strengths to create and lead worthwhile lives. They find moral clarity through a confluence of fate and nature, manage to hold fast to it (most of the time) and become beacons for the rest of us. Elie Wiesel was one of these people.

When you come into the presence of one of these heroes and pay attention, your universe within expands. This is what happened to me when I unexpectedly walked into the world of Elie Wiesel, a man who I only knew as a character in his first book, *Night*, the searing account of the horrors he had witnessed and endured in Auschwitz and Buchenwald as a teenager.

Although *Night* was written before I was born, I didn't read it in middle school or high school like many young people do today. In my youth, the Holocaust was still relatively unexamined, certainly in my house, where my father forbade us from buying German-made products, and we were haunted by an unspoken anxiety accumulated over centuries of persecution.

Books were my link to understanding the past, and my first inkling of what had taken place in the Holocaust came from *The Diary of Anne Frank*, the only volume about the subject assigned to schoolchildren of my era. Through it, we peered into the life of one extraordinary and resilient girl and her terrifying existence. But *The Diary of Anne Frank* did not take us directly into the concentration camps where millions perished.

Night did, and when I devoured it years later, I was swept away by the power of Elie's voice. That reading was a major factor in my decision to take over *Moment* in 2004. Elie had founded the magazine with Leonard "Leibel" Fein in 1975 to be a home for conversation among America's Jews. I believed that an independent magazine founded by two literary lions of the Jewish world should endure, and I hoped I would be able to inject fresh thinking, civility and a welcoming inclusivity into an increasingly polarized Jewish community.

Shortly afterward, I made a pilgrimage to Boston to meet both Leibel and Elie. Elie was then a professor at Boston University. After being ushered into his office, I introduced myself—and then found I could barely understand him. His spoken voice was whisper-like and his thick European accent difficult to decipher.

Once I grew accustomed to how he spoke, I learned that he and Leibel had named *Moment* for *Der Moment*, a popular Yiddish independent Warsaw daily founded in 1910 that, along with the lives of some of its editors, was extinguished by the Nazis after they invaded Poland in 1939. *Der Moment* was distributed throughout Eastern Europe, and Elie's father, Shlomo Wiesel, was a devoted reader in the family's hometown of Sighet, Romania. Elie, who studied at a yeshiva, never so much as touched the newspaper since he considered it—and the secular world it represented—off-limits. Yet when he emerged from the Holocaust and could no longer envision following a traditional religious life path, he thought of *Der Moment*. It inspired him to become a journalist. Years later, it also stirred him to establish a magazine. By naming it *Moment*, he and Leibel continued *Der Moment*'s legacy in a new time and on a different continent.

As years went by, Elie and I became friends. Sometimes we talked about *Moment*. He loved how the magazine carried on the torch of Jewish culture and expressed the tumult of Jewish thought, much as *Der Moment* had. He often told me he was proud of my work and said it was *bashert* ("intended" in Hebrew) that I had become the steward of *Moment*. He challenged me to write more and to trust my instincts and heart.

We bonded over writing. Elie saw himself first and

foremost as a writer, and that is how he wanted to be remembered. He chose his words with care, imbuing them with strength and beauty. But it is his moral clarity that will make his work endure for the ages. That clarity didn't come to him overnight. In the years after the Holocaust, he and other survivors—as well as historians—struggled to come to terms with what had taken place and to move forward, while remembering and remaining vigilant.

When he cofounded *Moment*, Elie was not yet a household name. By the time I met him, he was recognized as the leading voice of the survivors of the Holocaust. Most of us will never forget the day in April 1985 when Elie famously stood up to President Ronald Reagan, urging him to cancel a planned visit to a German cemetery where Nazis were buried.

I can never forget that Elie's voice was forged in suffering and shaped, largely, through the process of writing *Night*, and many other books, articles and speeches. It was a voice born from contradictions: He was a modern man steeped in the old Jewish world. Although he wrestled with God, he was a Jew who observed in memory of his family and who felt the soaring joys and haunting sounds of Jewish music in his soul. He craved the solitude of writing, yet he thrived on personal connections with people. He was serious but had a mischievous side that I came to love. He cared about Jews and he cared about all people, reminding us to never be indifferent to suffering. Elie never limited his concerns to anti-Semitism but instead challenged us to transcend prejudice of all kinds. He believed that humanity can learn and evolve and move beyond hatred based on

"Elie saw himself first and foremost as a writer, and that is how he wanted to be remembered. He chose his words with care, imbuing them with strength and beauty. But it is his moral clarity that will make his work endure for the ages."

"That place, Mr. President, is not your place," he said firmly during a White House ceremony where he was awarded the Congressional Gold Medal of Honor, the highest honor that the United States gives to civilians. "The issue here is not politics," he told President Reagan, "but good and evil. And we must never confuse them. For I have seen the SS at work. And I have seen their victims. They were my friends. They were my parents."

Those words propelled him into the public consciousness, and when Elie was awarded the Nobel Peace Prize the following year, the Nobel citation described him in prophetic terms. "Wiesel is a messenger to mankind," it said. "His message is one of peace, atonement and human dignity. His belief that the forces fighting evil in the world can be victorious is a hard-won belief."

religion, skin color, gender or ethnicity.

We at *Moment* have produced this book in the hope that Elie will not just be remembered for his tragic youth or as a famous person whose name you think you should know or as a one-dimensional super hero. Through the writings, reflections and photographs found on these pages, we want you to experience the breadth of Elie's values and passions and the multitude of ways in which he made a difference.

We believe that it is critical to keep Elie's memory alive at a time when anti-Semitism and prejudice of all kinds in the United States and Europe are once again on the rise, and the lessons he taught have been called into question.

I miss my gracious friend. He expanded my universe, and I hope this book will bring him into yours.

Never shall I forget that night, the first night in camp, that turned my life into one long night seven times sealed.

Never shall I forget that smoke.

Never shall I forget the small faces of the children whose bodies I saw transformed into smoke under a silent sky.

Never shall I forget those flames that consumed my faith forever.

Never shall I forget the nocturnal silence that deprived me for all eternity of the desire to live.

Never shall I forget those moments that murdered my God and my soul and turned my dreams to ashes.

Never shall I forget those things, even were I condemned to live as long as God Himself.

Never.

ELIE WIESEL
NIGHT

An Extraordinary Life

A Visual History

1928

Eliezer "Elie" Wiesel (center) was born on September 30 in Sighet, a town in Transylvania in Romania located near the border of Hungary. His parents were Sarah Feig (top center) and Shlomo Wiesel; both were active in the Jewish community. He had two older sisters, Beatrice (left) and Hilda (right); his younger sister Tzipora was born in 1937. The Wiesel family was multilingual but spoke Yiddish at home. Elie's parents encouraged him to study Hebrew, Torah and Talmud. As a child, he was deeply observant.

1933

Adolf Hitler was named Chancellor of Germany on January 30, after the Nazi Party became the largest political party in Parliament. A few months after seizing control of the government, the first official concentration camp, Dachau, was opened near Munich. On May 10, students tossed more than 25,000 volumes of "un-German" books into bonfires, presaging an era of state censorship and control over culture. Two years later, the Nuremberg Laws stripped Jews of German citizenship and prohibited them from marrying Germans.

1938–1939

On November 9-10, nearly 100 Jews were killed, and synagogues, Jewish businesses and Jewish homes were destroyed on what became known as Kristallnacht, "the night of broken glass," a government-organized pogrom against Jews in Germany, Austria and parts of Czechoslovakia. On September 1, 1939, World War II began when Germany invaded Poland, and Great Britain and France declared war on Germany. Soon after, Jews in German-occupied Poland were ordered to wear armbands displaying the Star of David and the first Polish Jewish ghetto was established.

1940–1942

Germany quickly conquered France, Norway, Denmark, Belgium, Luxembourg and the Netherlands. Romania was forced to cede Elie's hometown of Sighet to Hungary, which along with Romania and Slovakia joined the German-Italian Axis alliance. Meanwhile, not far from Krakow, Poland, a concentration camp was established that would become known as Auschwitz. In 1942, Hungarian police rounded up and deported foreign Jews living in Sighet, including Moshe the Beadle, with whom Elie (seen here with his sister Tzipora and his mother) had studied Kabbalah.

1942–1944

Moshe the Beadle escaped and returned to Sighet to warn others that the Jews who had been deported had been shot to death in the forest, but no one, including Elie, believed him. In 1944, the Germans arrived in Sighet, forced the Jews to move into ghettos, and began several rounds of deportations. The family's former maid offered to hide them in her village, but the family turned down the offer. Elie and his family and other Hungarian Jews were transported to Auschwitz (seen above) in a packed cattle car.

1944–1945

At Auschwitz, Elie's mother and Tzipora were immediately sent to the gas chambers. Separated from Hilda and Beatrice, Elie and his father managed to stay together. On January 18, 1945, as the Allies closed in, inmates were sent on a harrowing death march to the Buchenwald concentration camp. On January 29, Elie's father died of dysentery at Buchenwald, leaving Elie an orphan at age 16. On April 11, the Allies declared victory and Buchenwald was liberated by the U.S. Third Army. Elie was freed.

1947

Elie and other child survivors were sent to Normandy, France, to be cared for by a Jewish organization. He was reunited with his older sisters, who also survived, after his sister Hilda saw his photograph in a newspaper. He learned French, and the next year, moved to Paris to study literature, psychology and philosophy at the Sorbonne. He became a journalist for the Yiddish weekly *Zion in Kamf*, a publication of the Irgun—the Jewish paramilitary underground group fighting the British in Palestine—and later for the French newspaper *L'Arche*.

1948–1952

Elie refused to write about or discuss his Holocaust experiences. He became a foreign correspondent, traveling to the new State of Israel for the first time aboard the ship *Negba*. Assigned to write a series on new immigrants for *L'Arche*, he traveled through Israel conducting interviews and perfecting his Hebrew. In 1952, he became the Parisian correspondent for the Israeli newspaper *Yediot Aharanot,* launching a career that would take him throughout Europe and to India, Canada, South America and the United States.

1954–1955

Writer and Nobel Laureate Francois Mauriac convinced Elie to break his silence about his experiences and write about the Holocaust. Mauriac later said that Elie's gaze reminded him "of Lazarus risen from the dead yet still held captive in the somber regions into which he had strayed, stumbling over desecrated corpses." The following year, while on assignment in Brazil, Elie composed an 862-page manuscript in Yiddish, called *Un di velt hot geshvign (And the World Was Silent)*.

La Nuit:
First draft

an unpublished
chapter —

1956

An Argentinian Jewish publisher issued a 254-page version of *Un di velt hot geshvign* (above). With Mauriac's encouragement, Elie further edited the book and translated it into French, but was unable to find a publisher. Later that year, he moved to New York City to become *Yediot Aharanot*'s United Nations correspondent. Shortly after his arrival, he was struck by a taxicab in Times Square. He was hospitalized for months and nearly died from his injuries.

confiance générale. Son petit lui
main.

Le crépuscule commença à empl...
Nous nous mîmes à manger nos de...
visions. A dix heures du soir, ch...
cha une position convenable pou...
un peu, et bientôt tout le mor...
Soudain :

– Le feu ! L'incendie ! Regardez,

Réveillés en sursaut, nous nous ...
à la fenêtre. Nous l'avions crue, cette
ne fût-ce qu'un instant. Mais il n'y ...
que la nuit obscure. La honte dans...
regagnâmes notre place, rongés par
gré nous. Comme elle continuait à ...
nous remîmes à la battre et c'est à ...
que nous réussîmes à la faire taire.

Le responsable de notre wagon ap...
cier allemand qui se promenait sur...
demandant qu'on transportât notre...
wagon-hôpital.

– Patience, répondit l'autre, pati...

DOCUMENTS

ELIE WIESEL

LA NUIT

Préface de François Mauriac
de l'Académie française

☆m

LES ÉDITIONS DE MINUIT

oublié l'existence de mac...
dain, nous entendîmes un h...

...rdez ! Regardez le feu !
...lez !

... train s'était arrêté, nous v...
...mmes sortir d'une haute ch...
...l noir.

...ächter s'était tue d'elle-mê...
...devenue muette, indifféré...
... regagné son coin.

...ons les flammes dans la nuit...
...ble flottait dans l'air. Souc...
...vrirent. De curieux personna...
...rayées, de pantalons noirs,...
...wagon. Dans leurs mains,...
...e et un bâton. Ils se mire...
...: et à gauche, avant de crier
...nde descend ! Laissez tout c
...!

...es dehors. Je jetai un der...
...ame Schächter. Son petit gar

1958

Elie published an abridged version of his French manuscript, which he titled *La Nuit* (*Night*). He dedicated the book to the memory of his parents and Tzipora. In 1960, the book was cut further and appeared for the first time in English. Although it was critically acclaimed, *Night* was not a best-seller: The original print run of 3,000 took three years to sell out. The book would eventually be translated into 35 languages and become mandatory reading in schools around the world.

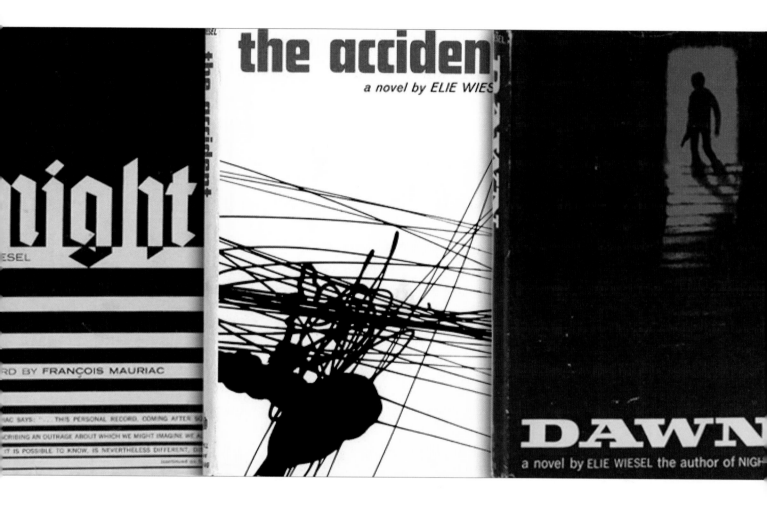

1960–1961

Following *Night*, Elie published his first novel, *Dawn*, the second installment in a trilogy. *Dawn* centers around Holocaust survivor Elisha, 18, who moves to the British Mandate of Palestine to join the Irgun, and is tasked with executing a British officer at dawn. A year later, Elie completed the trilogy with *Day* (initially called *The Accident* in English), a fictionalized account of his taxi accident and recovery: In it, he reflects on his own survival and on the death of family and friends in the Holocaust.

1963–1964

Elie became an American citizen, and a year later, returned to Sighet for the first time since the war and visited his childhood home (above). He wrote the novel *The Town Beyond the Wall*, about a young survivor who travels behind the Iron Curtain to visit his hometown in order to find and confront the townspeople who stood by when the Jews were deported, but is arrested as a foreign agent and imprisoned. Elie's writing began to win awards.

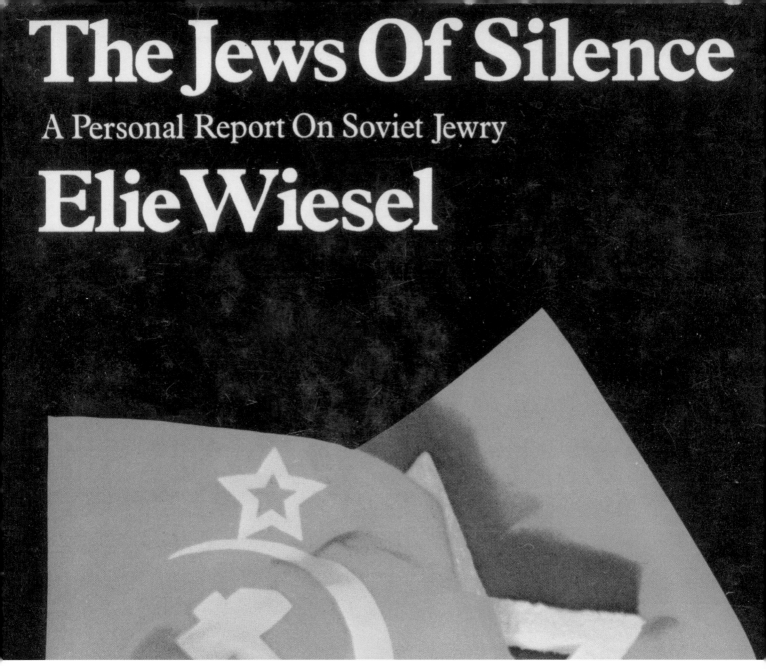

The Jews Of Silence

A Personal Report On Soviet Jewry

Elie Wiesel

1965

Elie traveled to the Soviet Union on an assignment from the Israeli newspaper *Haaretz* to investigate the plight of Jews trapped behind the Iron Curtain. In 1966, he published his first book on a topic other than the Holocaust, *The Jews of Silence: A Personal Report on Soviet Jewry*. It drew attention to the struggle of Soviet Jews and helped inspire the American Jewish community to take up their cause.

1968

Elie won the prestigious French literary award, the *Prix Medicis*, for *A Beggar in Jerusalem.* The novel is about a Holocaust survivor who rushes to Israel after the Six-Day War to visit the newly reunited city of Jerusalem and encounters madmen and ghosts from his past. The following year, Elie married Marion Erster Rose, who was born in Austria and escaped the Nazis by fleeing to Belgium and Switzerland. She became his primary translator.

1972

Marion gave birth to their son, Shlomo Elisha Wiesel, named for Elie's father. Elie was appointed the Distinguished Professor of Judaic Studies at the City College of the City University of New York. At the time, the Holocaust was still rarely discussed outside survivor circles. Many of his students were the children of survivors who opened up to him about their families' experiences. He encouraged them to tell their stories.

VOL. I NO. 1 SIVAN TAMMUZ 5735 MAY JUNE 1975 TWO DOLLARS'

MOMENT
THE NEW MAGAZINE FOR AMERICA'S JEWS ✱ FOUNDED BY LEONARD FEIN AND ELIE WIESEL

Premiere Issue

A Song for Women, in Five Questions
Susan Dworkin

The New Jewish Right
Harold Schulweis

Remembering
Elie Wiesel

Jacob Schiff and My Uncle Ben Daynovsky
Calvin Trillin

Fiction / David Stern
Poetry / Joel Rosenberg

ISRAEL:

Pride and Paradox: An Exchange / Robert Alter / Shlomo Avineri
Can Israel Win Another War? / Drew Middleton
The Real Threat of the P.L.O. / Stephen Philip Cohen

1975

Together with Leonard Fein, Elie founded *Moment Magazine*, named in memory of the independent Yiddish newspaper *Der Moment,* published in Warsaw from 1910 to 1939. As a yeshiva boy, the newspaper had been off-limits to Elie, but he had fond memories of his father reading it. *Der Moment* shut down when the Nazis marched into Warsaw in 1939. His memory of *Der Moment* was one of the inspirations for his becoming a journalist.

1976

Elie joined the faculty of Boston University with a joint appointment in the religion and philosophy departments. He was named the Andrew W. Mellon Professor in the Humanities. Every fall he taught two courses on literature and memory. He only once taught a course on the Holocaust and disliked it so much that he never did it again. Elie loved teaching and remained on the faculty until he retired in 2013.

1978–1980

President Jimmy Carter (left) created the President's Commission on the Holocaust, charging it to find an appropriate way to remember the Holocaust in the nation's capital. He appointed Elie as its chairman. The commission solicited suggestions from American citizens and traveled to Holocaust-era sites and memorials in Europe. It submitted its report in 1979, and in 1980 Elie became the chairman of the United States Holocaust Memorial Museum.

1985

Chartered by a unanimous act of Congress, the federal government provided 1.9 acres of land adjacent to the national mall in Washington, DC for the site of the United States Holocaust Memorial Museum. On October 16, two milk cartons containing soil and ashes from a number of concentration camps and killing centers were buried on the site to symbolize the museum's mission. Elie participated in the groundbreaking ceremony.

1985

At an April 15th press conference at Hebrew Union College-Jewish Institute of Religion in New York City, Elie spoke out against President Ronald Reagan's plans to visit Bitburg, a German military cemetery where members of Hitler's elite Waffen SS were buried. Other survivors and second-generation leaders also participated.

1985

On April 19, Elie was awarded the Congressional Gold Medal of Achievement by President Reagan. At the ceremony, Elie delivered an impassioned plea for Reagan to cancel his impending visit to Bitburg. "That place, Mr. President, is not your place," he said. "Your place is with the victims of the SS." Elie's speech garnered worldwide attention.

1986–1987

On December 10, Elie received the Nobel Peace Prize in Oslo, Norway. In this photo taken shortly afterward, he is seen with his wife, Marion, and their son, Elisha, and Egil Aarvik, the chairman of the Norwegian Nobel Committee. The following year, Elie and Marion established The Elie Wiesel Foundation for Humanity, an organization to fight intolerance, injustice and indifference to these conditions wherever they exist.

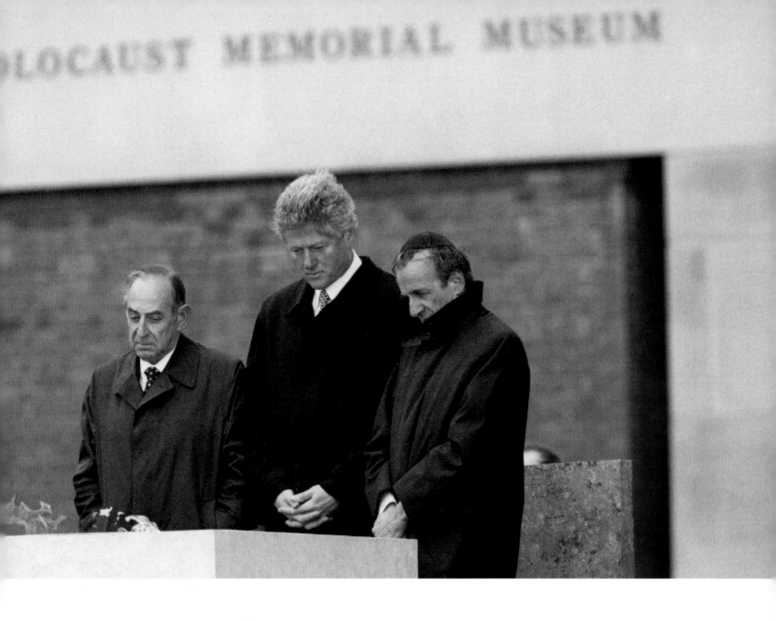

1993

Dedication ceremonies for the United States Holocaust Memorial Museum took place on April 22—Yom Hashoah, Holocaust Remembrance Day. Elie spoke as did President Bill Clinton, Israeli President Chaim Herzog and Harvey Meyerhoff, chairman of the United States Holocaust Memorial Council. In his speech, Elie raised the alarm about mass killings in the former Yugoslavia. Several days later, on April 26, the museum officially opened to the public.

2000–2003

Elie maintained that the genocide of Armenians in the Ottoman Empire during World War I was an incontestable historical fact and urged the United States Congress and other governments to recognize it as such. In 2003, Elie addressed survivors and thousands of their family members at the Tribute to Holocaust Survivors at the United States Holocaust Memorial Museum—the last major assembly of the Holocaust survivor generation. (He spoke at all major survivor gatherings including the first large-scale one in Jerusalem in 1981.)

2004–2006

As chairman of the International Commission on the Holocaust in Romania, Elie delivered a report blaming Romanian authorities for the mass Jewish killings in their country during the Holocaust. He also spoke out against ethnic violence in Sudan at the Darfur Emergency Summit in New York, invoking the biblical commandment, "Thou shall not stand idly by the shedding of the blood of thy fellow man." In 2006, Elie and actor and humanitarian activist George Clooney addressed the UN Security Council about Darfur.

2009

In June, Elie returned to the Buchenwald concentration camp in Germany with U.S. President Barack Obama, German Chancellor Angela Merkel and Holocaust survivor Bertrand Herz. "If these trees could talk," Elie told the group as they entered the camp, adding that he felt as if he were visiting his father's grave, which he described as being "somewhere in the sky." In his remarks, he lamented that "the world hasn't learned" from the Holocaust. "Had the world learned, there would have been no Cambodia and no Rwanda and no Darfur and no Bosnia. Will the world ever learn?"

2012

Elie published his last book, *Open Heart*. "I still believe in man in spite of man," he wrote in the memoir. "I believe in language even though it has been wounded, deformed, and perverted by the enemies of mankind. And I continue to cling to words because it is up to us to transform them into instruments of comprehension rather than contempt. It is up to us to choose whether we wish to use them to curse or to heal, to wound or to console." That year, Elie also traveled to Auschwitz with TV talk show host Oprah Winfrey, who had selected *Night* for her book club in 2006.

2016

Elie died on July 2 at his home in Manhattan. A private funeral was held at the Fifth Avenue Synagogue in New York. In a statement about Elie's legacy, President Obama said: "As a writer, a speaker, an activist and a thinker, he was one of those people who changed the world more as a citizen of the world than those who hold office or traditional positions of power. His life, and the power of his example, urges us to be better."

2016

Elie was laid to rest at Sharon Gardens in Westchester County, New York. A simple stone marks his grave. "I have learned two lessons in my life: first, there are no sufficient literary, psychological or historical answers to human tragedy, only moral ones," he once said. "Second, just as despair can come to one another only from other human beings, hope, too, can be given to one only by other human beings."

Many Legacies

36 Reflections

Yosef Abramowitz

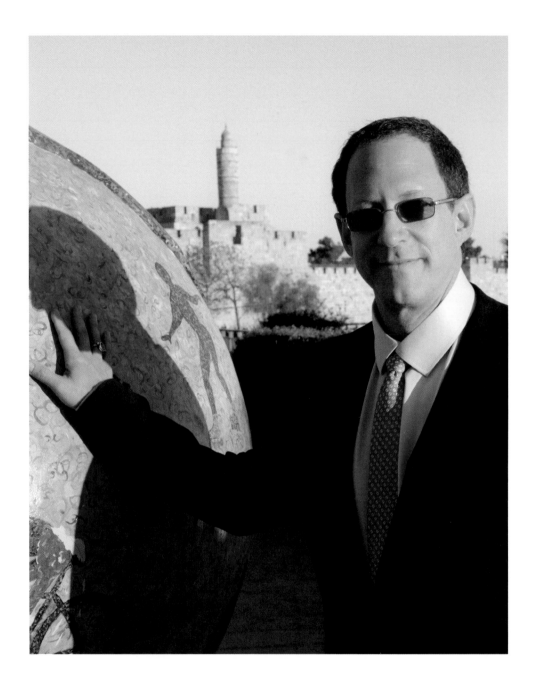

Yosef Abramowitz is the CEO of Energiya Global Capital.
In 2006 he cofounded Arava Power Company, which
developed Israel's first commercial solar field.

> "I think in an age of growing religious extremism and polarization in Jewish life, we are going to miss Professor Wiesel's example and the center of moral gravity that he represented."

I always called him Professor Wiesel, even when we were friends, because he had a different air about him. I was a student and the leader of the anti-apartheid movement at Boston University, where Wiesel was a professor, and I finally got up the guts to walk into his office and sign up for his course. When I walked in, Martha Hauptman, his longtime assistant, looked up and said, "What took you so long?"

I had been a controversial figure on campus, as a Jew and a Zionist leading the anti-apartheid movement, and the president of the university was against me. Wiesel would see me in his office, and he would encourage me to keep coming and remind me that it is important to be on the right side of history as a Jew. Even when the university was trying to expel me, he was doing everything to strengthen my fortitude and moral outrage.

He loved teaching above all else. It gave him inspiration. He raised so many students, made time for his students. He was just like the Lubavitcher Rebbe meeting one-on-one with his Hasidim. Hundreds, maybe thousands, feel cherished among his students.

I don't think anybody else in Jewish life did as good a job as Professor Wiesel of balancing the particular and the universal, of affirming the centrality and depth of Jewish values without giving in to narrow parochialism. No one had as much depth, nor a wider view of humanity, and he did all that as a Jew. Professor Wiesel felt it was his responsibility to be a bridge between the Jewish people and humanity. I think in an age of growing religious extremism and polarization in Jewish life, we are going to miss his example and the center of moral gravity that he represented.

Gerard Araud

Gerard Araud is Ambassador of France to the United States. He was Ambassador to Israel and permanent representative to the United Nations.

"Today, Wiesel's work still resonates in France's collective memory. Indeed, *Night* remains a seminal book; it continues to raise awareness about the Holocaust and the concentration camps."

There was an unwavering bond between Elie Wiesel and France. It can be best summarized by Wiesel's praise of the French language in a 2008 interview with the magazine *Le Nouvel Observateur*: "French is both the language of intelligence and a challenge."

After his release from the Buchenwald camp in 1945, Wiesel was raised as an orphan in French public institutions in Vendôme and Versailles. He studied at the Sorbonne University and then became a journalist and a translator. Paris seduced him and influenced him both as a journalist and a philosopher. In Paris, he met his close friend and mentor, Nobel Laureate François Mauriac. Mauriac convinced Wiesel to write about his experiences in the death camps. That book later became Wiesel's autobiography, *Night*. In 1956, Wiesel left France for the United States, but he retained his passion for the French language and always spoke of his "profound link to the French culture" and a "loyalty to the classical style." "This language chose me," he declared in a 2010 interview with the French newspaper *Le Monde*.

Today, Wiesel's work still resonates in France's collective memory. Indeed, *Night* remains a seminal book; it continues to raise awareness about the Holocaust and the concentration camps. Wiesel had many close friends among the French, including President François Mitterrand and Culture Minister Jack Lang. In collaboration with them, in 1992 Wiesel founded the Universal Academy of Cultures. This organization brings together luminaries from the fields of literature, science, economics, the law and the arts to study ways to combat intolerance, xenophobia, racism and anti-Semitism. Wiesel relentlessly raised his voice against indifference and oppression. It is our duty to make sure that it does not now fall silent.

Nahum Barnea

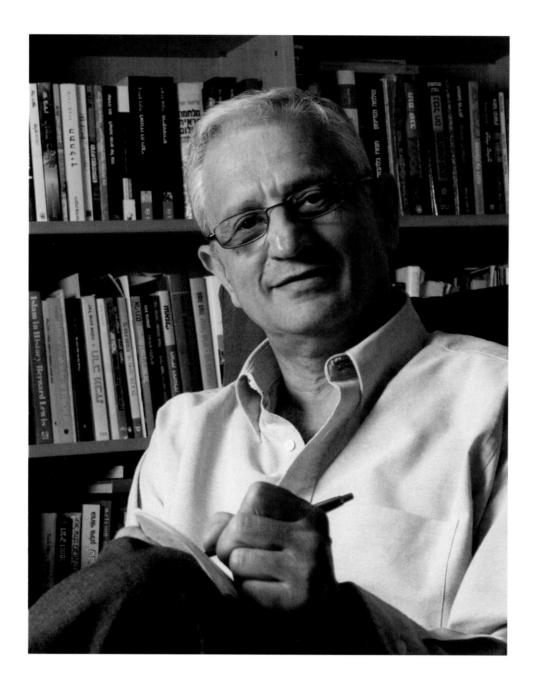

Nahum Barnea is the chief columnist of the Israeli newspaper *Yediot Aharanot* and an investigative journalist. He received the Israel Prize in 2007.

> "When Elie opened his mouth, Israelis believed that the Holocaust was speaking directly to them. When people talked about Elie they talked about the Holocaust. He was the Holocaust."

After serving as its Paris correspondent, Elie was assigned to be the *Yediot Aharanot* correspondent in New York, focusing mainly on the United Nations, which in the 1950s was a very important assignment in the Israeli media. He was very active. He wrote a lot of pieces, and his Hebrew was perfect, not because he had lived in Israel, but because he was a good student and had studied Hebrew in childhood. He spoke Hebrew without a foreign accent. It was quite amazing.

About ten years ago, he called me and said that he enjoyed reading my work in *Yediot*. He liked my style. I was surprised. We started to exchange calls because he was interested in life in Israel. He was a curious man, a very open man and he knew a lot. This is how we became friendly.

He had a commitment never to criticize Israel. I would say, 'Why, when you can influence Israel positively by talking about mistakes we made?' He always said, "No, because I have never lived in Israel, I don't have the right to criticize Israel."

His image was different in Israel than in the United States. For the rest of the world, Elie went beyond the Holocaust. But in Israel he was recognized almost entirely by the Holocaust. When he opened his mouth, Israelis believed that the Holocaust was speaking directly to them. When people talked about Elie they talked about the Holocaust. He was the Holocaust.

I have a story that is unbelievable. I took my son to Auschwitz after he finished the army. It was the eve of Rosh Hashanah, in Auschwitz, when we stood under the sign that read *arbeit macht frei*, and my cell phone rang. I hesitated as to whether to push the green button or not. I thought that I should switch the phone off. But I pushed the green button, and who was on the phone but Elie Wiesel. We had a tradition to call one another on the eves of Jewish holidays. I said, "Elie you won't believe this, I am at Auschwitz with my son. What should I do with my son here?" He said, "Don't speak. Keep silent. Don't explain. Let him go by himself." And this is what I did. I kept a full yard distance between my son and me. I am not sure it was good or bad advice. Elie told me that he did the same thing with his son. He wanted him to face Auschwitz by himself.

Elie would not say it like this, but my lesson from Elie is that Israel cannot stand on the wrong side of the global human rights debate. The way you treat people is very important. The Holocaust taught us that we should not be on wrong side regarding human rights. I don't forget the other lesson it taught—that the Jewish people should be strong enough to deter its enemies. In Elie's view, these two points were not contradictions.

Joseph Berger

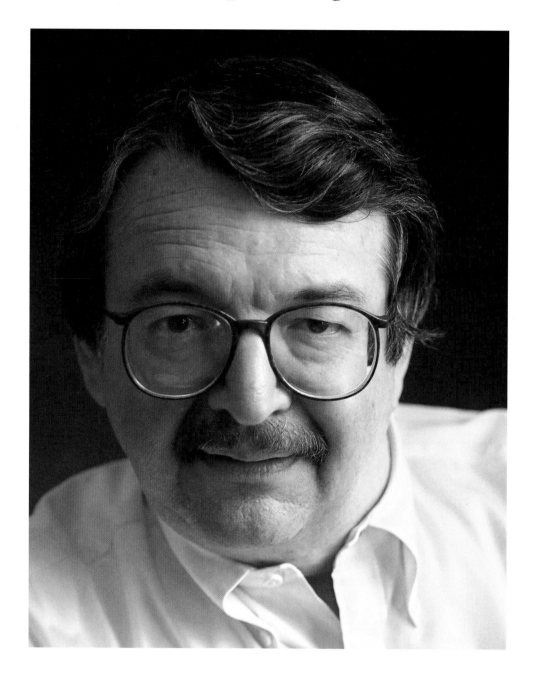

Joseph Berger has written a biography of Elie Wiesel for
Yale University Press. He was a reporter and editor at
The New York Times for more than 30 years.

> "His furrowed, handsome face had a haunted, distracted look, as if he spoke to the Heavens. And yet those who knew him remark on how fundamentally down to earth he was."

Elie Wiesel had the aura of a prophet. He often spoke in mystical, paradoxical phrases about grand moral themes: the absence of God during the Holocaust, the evils of silence and indifference in the face of cruelty. His furrowed, handsome face had a haunted, distracted look, as if he spoke to the Heavens. And yet those who knew him remark how fundamentally down to earth he was. He loved to join friends in singing the Hasidic and Yiddish melodies he had grown up with in Sighet, Romania. The first time I saw him up close, in 1973, he and a fellow survivor, Sigmund Strochlitz, were on a plane headed to Israel during the Yom Kippur War, two shoeless Jews tenderly humming nostalgic melodies because of the tribal feelings set off by that imperiled moment. Though invited to the most prestigious courts, he remained a man of modest tastes; his son, Elisha, told me he preferred instant coffee to the brewed variety because that was what he had grown accustomed to in his more hardscrabble years. Indeed, we forget that he was, beyond a global icon, a husband and father, one who for some years had to grapple with a son rebelling at having to grow up with a global icon.

Yet, Elie Wiesel managed to become the spokesman for the survivors of the 20th century's most disgraceful outrage. As I wrote in an obituary for the *Times*, "in the aftermath of the Germans' systematic massacre of the Jews of Europe, no voice had emerged to drive home the enormity of what had happened and how it had changed mankind's conception of itself and of God. But by the sheer force of his personality and his gift for the haunting phrase, Mr. Wiesel... exhumed the Holocaust from the burial ground of the history books." Moreover, he enlarged that legacy to become the conscience of mankind wherever genocide and oppression reared.

In 1986, after the press conference that followed the announcement of his Nobel Peace Prize, I asked him how he had recovered from the emotional wounds of his war experience, and he replied that he went "from despair to despair" and even now sometimes battled with those feelings. "But," he said, "we have to go into the despair and go beyond it, by working and doing for somebody else, by using it for something else."

"I felt that having survived I owe something to the dead," he said. "That was their obsession, to be remembered."

More than anyone else, Elie Wiesel made sure the six million would be remembered.

Michael Berenbaum

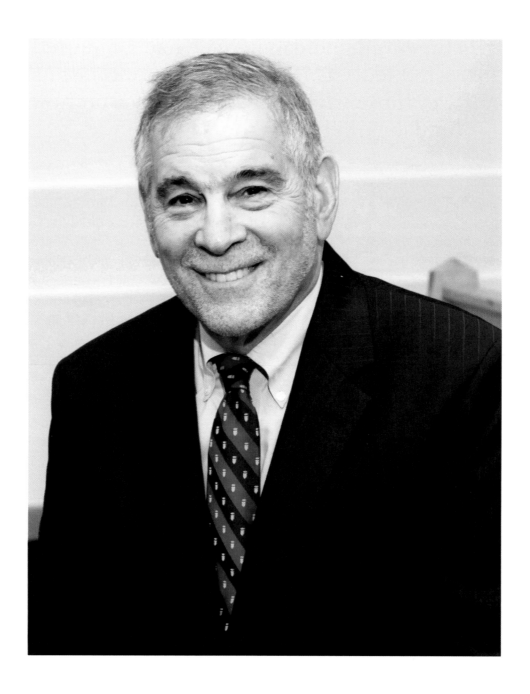

Michael Berenbaum is Director of the Sigi Ziering Institute and a Professor of Jewish Studies at American Jewish University in Los Angeles. He was founding project director of the United States Holocaust Memorial Museum.

"The language in Elie's early books gave all of us a new way to wrestle with God, to confront God and to speak with the God of Auschwitz. Elie showed us the abyss, but he never fell into it."

When Elie Wiesel left this world in July of 2016, he was a man sated with honors; a Nobel Laureate, he was also, as Leonard Fein once described him, the "conscience laureate" of the Jewish people, admired, cherished, revered and respected. Courted by presidents and prime ministers, cardinals, ministers and rabbis, he was not only prized by the economic, political and social elite but venerated by ordinary men and women worldwide. Like Albert Einstein before him, he—as a non-citizen of Israel—was offered the presidency of the State of Israel because he would bring prestige to the office, and like Einstein, he could—and he did—say no.

So it is difficult to remember that Elie Wiesel was a dissident, someone comfortable with opposing official policies. He was an outspoken critic of American Judaism and espoused positions that were unpopular at a time when consensus was the operative norm. He confronted serious opposition before ultimately succeeding in making his agenda become the agenda of the American Jewish community.

He had a particular view of America and American Judaism, especially in his early years. Unlike most survivors who first experienced freedom in the United States and rebuilt their lives there, Elie's journey took him to France. He wrote: "I owe France my secular education, my language and my career as a writer. Liberated from Buchenwald, it was in France that I found compassion and humanity. It was in France that I found generosity and friendship. It was in France that I discovered the other side, the brighter side of mankind." Frenchmen who lived through the Shoah in France are far less charitable. Elie was critical of American Jewish complacency during the war and of American Jewish leadership's reticence to risk on behalf of their beleaguered brethren. Even his fictionalized American Jewish characters lacked the depth and sophistication of the European ones.

Elie believed that the Holocaust was the centerpiece of the contemporary Jewish experience, an event of transformative importance, dare one say transcendent significance. It was the counter-testimony to another formative event in Jewish history—Sinai, the moment when Jews came face-to-face with the anti-God and the anti-man.

Fifteen years later when he was called upon to recommend to the president an appropriate national memorial to the Holocaust, American Jewish leaders were reluctant to join him. The funds, they argued, could be better used in support of Israel and of federations or even for Jewish education. Who needs a museum on the Mall? Who would be interested? Would it provoke anti-Semitism? Why not build it in New York by the Jews and for the Jews? The Israelis argued that Jews already had Yad Vashem. They feared that it would become a rival, taking away from them the exclusive mantel of the Holocaust or that it would become an agent of dejudaization.

For Elie the Holocaust posed more questions than answers: Where was God? The Jewish narrative had changed. Jewish tradition teaches that all Jews stood at Sinai and heard the divine revelation commanding that love of God be demonstrated in responsibility toward one another. All Jews stood at Auschwitz seeing face-to-face the anti-God and the anti-humanity.

Elie wrestled with God. He was a conflicted soul. Then on Yom Kippur Eve, one year in the 1990s, he finally made peace with God. On one level he was a

believer, on another—especially earlier in his life—he was a disbeliever. Later he lost that fierceness; he found reconciliation. His language in his early books gave all of us a new way to wrestle with God, to confront God and to speak with the God of Auschwitz. Wiesel showed us the abyss, but he never fell into it.

Elie was one of the early figures in the Soviet Jewry movement. He began his efforts in the early 1960s with two trips to the Soviet Union, writing his book *The Jews of Silence*. He came back from the Soviet Union convinced that almost a half-century after the Bolshevik revolution, Soviet Jews wanted to remain Jews and to maintain not only their contact with, but their allegiance to, the Jewish people. Communism had not succeeded in eradicating their Jewish identity, which he saw in religious terms, but which we now know was national rather than religious. Furthermore, Elie argued that we—American Jews—were the Jews of silence.

nonsensical answer to that; he would say that he wasn't worthy. The reality was that his task was to be a mediating figure and to represent Jews around the world. That didn't play well in the rough and tumble politics of Israel. Furthermore, Elie was a "Jew" before he was an "Israeli." Israelis questioned why he chose to write *Night* in French when his Hebrew was so good. He also didn't write it in Yiddish even though Yiddish was his native tongue. He chose to write it in an "adopted" language, an international tongue. In the end, he did not have the same influence in Israel that he had in the rest of the world, Further, the influence he did have there was a result of his high status among Jews in the Diaspora.

Elie transformed our understanding of survivors. At first Holocaust victims were considered refugees, the latest in a long string of Jews who suffered elsewhere and needed a haven. They were seen by many as damaged goods. Their survival was often regarded

"Over time, Elie won his plea for survivors, and they have been transformed from people who were to be pitied into symbols of resilience and strength."

It was within the capacity of free Jews in the United States, throughout the Diaspora and even in Israel to free Soviet Jewry if only we dared, if only we cared.

Elie was opposed by some in Israel interested in advancing diplomatic relations with the Soviet Union, which were not severed until after the 1967 war. American Jewish leadership viewed the cause as hopeless, and they perceived themselves as powerless to affect such a global issue. Many insisted on quiet diplomacy and an underground movement to protect Jews. Elie was not a lone voice—he was not yet Elie Wiesel, a man of international influence—but he was a significant voice and he persisted. Consider the results.

People would be surprised to learn that Israel was one of the most difficult places for Elie. Publicly, Elie was one of Israel's most ardent defenders. Yet the Israelis questioned why he didn't live there. Elie would give a

as an accusation: What did you do to survive that others did not? In Israel some were called *sabonikim*, soaps. There and elsewhere the victims were accused of going like sheep to the slaughter.

Over time, Elie won his plea for survivors, and they have been transformed from people who were to be pitied into symbols of resilience and strength. They have come to be regarded as witnesses and teachers, speaking to this generation and beyond. They have spoken, and their words are a cry against indifference, a plea for tolerance and pluralism, for human values and human dignity, for democracy and the protection of human rights—and as a plea for Israel. He was their exemplar and the power of his voice elevated theirs.

His dissidence transformed the Jewish agenda. Had this been all he accomplished, *dayeinu*—it would have been sufficient.

Wolf Blitzer

Wolf Blitzer is CNN's lead political anchor and the host of *The Situation Room with Wolf Blitzer*.

"Elie Wiesel, the Holocaust survivor, the author, the activist, the humanitarian, never minced words, never shied away from recalling the brutality of the Holocaust."

It was April 22, 1993—a day I will always remember. At that time I was CNN's senior White House correspondent. My assignment for that day was to cover President Bill Clinton and other dignitaries at the historic opening of the United States Holocaust Memorial Museum in Washington, DC. In 1978, Elie Wiesel had been asked by President Jimmy Carter to help create a national Holocaust museum on the Washington Mall. Fifteen years later, the museum was finally ready for visitors from around the world to remember the Holocaust and to learn from it. Elie's words that day were and remain profound: "For the dead and the living, we must bear witness. For not only are we responsible for the memories of the dead, we are also responsible for what we are doing with those memories."

I was deeply moved by Elie's comments. I also remember that it was bitter cold and raining that day. Some thought that was bad because a sunny day would have been easier for the large crowd of people that had gathered outside. But as I watched the ceremony unfold, I thought the weather was appropriate. I suspect Elie did as well. Remembering the Holocaust is certainly not a happy occasion. I also remember thinking of my own grandparents on that day. I never knew them; all four were murdered during the Holocaust.

Elie Wiesel, the Holocaust survivor, the author, the activist, the humanitarian, never minced words, never shied away from recalling the brutality of the Holocaust. On that day as world leaders watched and listened, he said: "In Poland, SS officers used Jewish infants for target practice. The only emotion they ever showed was anger when they missed. In Kiev, an SS officer beheaded two Jewish children in front of their mother, who in her anguish, in prey of some mystical madness, held them close to her bosom and began to dance. In Romania, the Aryan guards hanged Jews on meat hooks and displayed them in butcher shops with signs, 'Kosher Meat.'"

The large crowd on the National Mall was silent as he spoke, tears flowed, including from members of Congress, foreign diplomats and most movingly, from Holocaust survivors who had gathered.

I want to thank Elie Wiesel again for making all of us remember and learn from that dreadful chapter in Jewish history. I was blessed to have met Elie on several occasions. I always emerged from our interviews smarter, as did our viewers. He was an inspiration in his soft-spoken way.

Sam E. Bloch

Sam E. Bloch (1924-2018) was President of the American Gathering of Jewish Holocaust Survivors and Their Descendants and of the World Federation of Bergen-Belsen Associations. He also chaired the United States Holocaust Memorial Council's Board of Advisors.

> "Whenever Elie would meet with survivors,
> he would always tell us 'Write your stories.'
> He believed passionately in the power of the written
> word as a permanent form of remembrance."

I first met Elie when he was a young journalist working in New York in the late 1950s. We developed a close friendship, bound by a deep understanding of each other's experiences as teenagers during the Holocaust. Having survived, our mission was to make the world remember our martyrs and to break the pervasive silence about the Shoah. We were both driven to ensure the remembrance of the destruction of our people under the Nazis and their collaborators and to educate the world about the ultimate consequences of anti-Semitism, intolerance, inhumanity and injustice.

During the 1950s and 1960s, the Jewish community and the larger world were disinterested in our experiences. There was a resounding silence that made us, the survivors, feel isolated and disregarded. As young people in our 20s and 30s, we were all creating new lives, new families, in new countries—but the scars of the Shoah were deeply embedded in our bodies, souls and hearts. Elie became our "voice" as the representative of our survivor generation.

Elie's writings recorded our memories and validated our identities as the surviving remnant, the *sheirit hapletah*, of European Jewry. He was always there to defend our perspective in order to sustain the integrity of Holocaust memory and combat all forms of revisionism and exploitation of the Shoah. For us, he was our shining light who became the conscience and guardian of the memory of the Jewish people.

We, the survivors, took great pride in all of Elie's achievements and his growing prominence.

We were at his side when he raised the consciousness of the world about the plight of Soviet Jewry, when he spoke out on behalf of Israel, when he alerted the world that Jews were in jeopardy in other parts of the world, and when he called for action against the genocides in Cambodia, Rwanda and Bosnia. We were with him when he opposed the obscene equation of the SS officers buried at Bitburg and the Jewish mass graves of Bergen Belsen. And we were present when he received the Nobel Prize, when this prominent recognition of a survivor of the Shoah brought us all a great sense of fulfillment.

I remember when Elie chaired President Carter's Commission on the Holocaust and we traveled together in 1979 to the Holocaust killing sites throughout Europe to produce a report that resulted in the creation of the U.S. Holocaust Memorial Museum. I will never forget how we walked, arm-in-arm, as we entered Auschwitz-Birkenau. It was traumatic to return to the places where our families were annihilated, but we strengthened each other with the shared memories that united us.

Whenever Elie would meet with survivors, he would always tell us, "Write your stories." He believed passionately in the power of the written word as a permanent form of remembrance. He told us that our testimonies would endure to educate and inspire future generations to remember those who perished through the words of those who survived to tell the world.

Sara Bloomfield

Sara Bloomfield is Director of the United States Holocaust
Memorial Museum, a position she has held since 1999.

"If you wanted to boil down everything to its essence with Elie, the biggest sin was indifference. He felt that indifference was a bigger sin than hate and evil."

Whether he was standing in front of a class, giving a speech, or meeting with people in the Middle East or Europe, wherever he was around the world, Elie Wiesel felt his role was to be a teacher. He would say that the United States Holocaust Memorial Museum was also a teacher. His role as an institution builder is under-recognized. It's very important to list this among his extraordinary legacies because, without Elie Wiesel, it is hard to imagine the Holocaust Remembrance Movement. And without him and that movement, it is hard to imagine that the United States Holocaust Memorial Museum would exist. As the head of the presidential commission to establish the museum and as its founding chairman, he had a very particular mission for the museum. And he was the only person who had the moral authority to envision and to articulate what became the soul of the museum.

In the early years of developing the museum, people struggled with the question, "Would it be Jewish, or would it be universal, and would the Holocaust lose some of its uniqueness?" It was Elie's vision, his moral clarity, his intellect and his eloquence that said it was both. The Holocaust was both a universal event—a cataclysm for all mankind—and a very specifically unique Jewish event. He called the museum a living memorial. Elie said, "It's our conviction that when any one people is targeted and engulfed in the fire, all humanity is engulfed." And this museum is really a museum about humanity. That did not at all diminish Jewish specificity, and it helped us shape how we communicated that Jewish specificity to very broad and diverse audiences.

If you wanted to boil down everything to its essence with Elie, the biggest sin was indifference. He felt that indifference was a bigger sin than hate and evil. So he himself had to lead his life that way. That meant speaking truth to power. The labels attributed to him—author, teacher, activist, thinker—are all under that idea of "voice." But for him, voice was action. Voice was using words to inspire, but also to always speak out on behalf of the voiceless, to give voice to them, whether they were the six million or the people in Sarajevo, to do for others what was not done for the Jews of Europe in the 1930s and 1940s.

Thomas Buergenthal

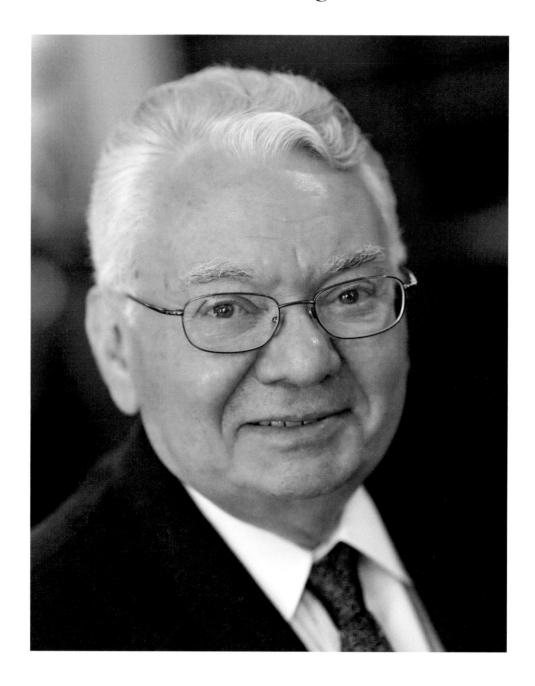

Thomas Buergenthal is a professor of comparative law and jurisprudence at the George Washington University Law School. He was a judge on the International Court of Justice.

"Elie didn't limit himself to the Holocaust. He realized that the lesson of the Holocaust, of his experience and that of those of us who went through it and survived, was that you had to fight and support those whose human rights have been violated—now and in the future."

Elie once told me that he and I were on the same death march out of Auschwitz in January of 1945. The death march was one of my worst camp experiences, an experience I always wanted to forget but never could. Neither could he, but that did not weaken his commitment to working and speaking for tolerance and human rights for all mankind.

Elie didn't limit himself to the Holocaust. He realized that the lesson of the Holocaust, of his experience and that of those of us who went through it and survived, was that you had to fight and support those whose human rights have been violated—now and in the future.

By his actions he legitimized the voice of the survivors to speak not only about the Holocaust, but also about improving human rights conditions in the world. His biggest accomplishment in my eyes was his work on the United States Holocaust Museum. We wouldn't have gotten to the place that we have today if Elie had not supported the idea that the museum should be a place for the dead and the living. Elie and I always believed that it was necessary for the museum to devote itself not only to the memory of those who died in the Holocaust, but also to trying to prevent future violations of human rights. He established a standard that the museum is still implementing by coming out with strong statements and having programs to educate people about genocide and human rights abuses.

Let us honor his memory by emulating him; it will make for a better world.

Joseph Ciechanover

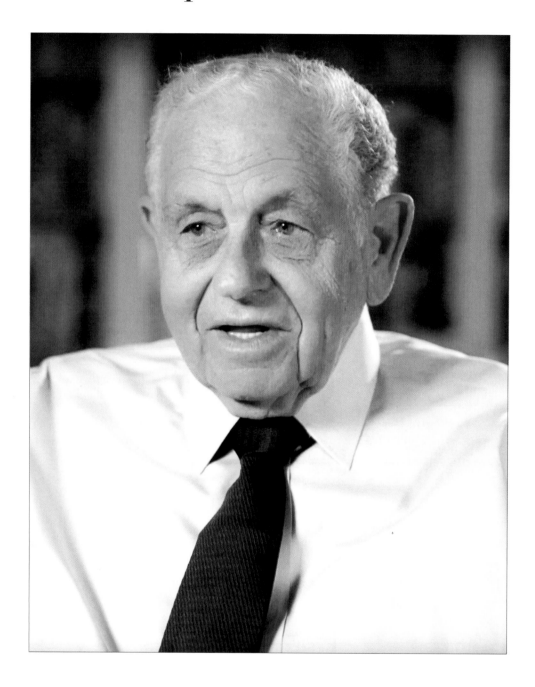

Joseph Ciechanover was Director General of the Ministry of Foreign Affairs of Israel. He served on Israel's Defense Mission to the United States and Canada and as general counsel to the Ministry of Defense.

"The legacy Elie left us is to not let the Holocaust of the Jewish people in the 20th century be forgotten or denied."

I knew Elie Wiesel for over 45 years. A mutual friend introduced us during one of my trips to New York. Since that time, we had a very close relationship. A week never passed without us speaking at least once on the telephone and exchanging views on current events.

Elie's spoken voice has now been silenced, but his words in the more than 50 books he wrote and speeches he delivered will always remain present.

The legacy he left us is to not let the Holocaust of the Jewish people in the 20th century be forgotten or denied.

Elie was a staunch defender of the State of Israel, fighting for its right to exist as a home for the Jewish people. It was inconceivable to him that Israel should be attacked for defending its right to exist.

Dani Dayan

Dani Dayan is the Consul General of Israel in New York. He was Chairman of the Yesha Council, an organization of municipal councils of Jewish settlements in the West Bank.

"We must know what happened, not just for future generations, but as a commitment to the victims. The child who was taken from Amsterdam to Auschwitz deserves to have us know how he died. Elie Wiesel contributed enormously to our knowledge of the Holocaust."

Elie Wiesel is well known and appreciated in Israel. He is a Jewish figure, not just an American-Jewish figure. For me, the Shoah is omnipresent. I believe that we have four main obligations concerning the Shoah.

The first is to mourn. For me, Yom HaShoah is the day on which we mourn. I weep on that day. The six million brothers who died deserve that.

The second is to know. And we must know what happened, not just for future generations, but as a commitment to the victims. The child who was taken from Amsterdam to Auschwitz deserves to have us know how he died. Elie Wiesel contributed enormously to our knowledge of the Holocaust.

The third, and perhaps the most difficult, is to try to feel. There is a passage in the Passover Haggadah, "In each and every generation, each person is obligated to see himself or herself as though he or she personally came forth from Egypt." Since World War II, each person should see himself or herself as if he or she was liberated from Auschwitz.

The fourth is to learn a lesson. Each person is entitled to his own lessons. Some lessons are universal; others are solely Jewish or very personal. As long as the lessons are sincere, they are all legitimate. My lesson from the Shoah is the need for a Jewish State.

Elie Wiesel was the reflection of, and the fulfillment of, all four of these. He was the face and the voice of the six million victims of the Shoah.

Patrick Desbois

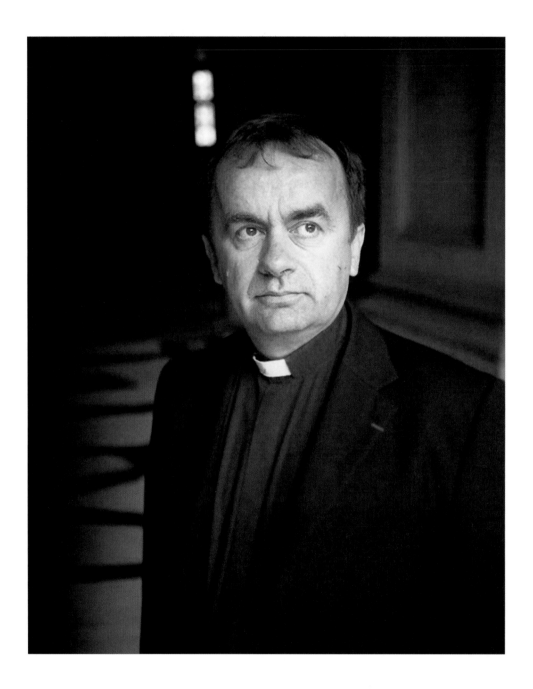

Patrick Desbois is a French Roman Catholic priest and founder of
Yahad-In Unum, an organization that locates and documents mass
graves of Jewish victims of the Nazis in Eastern Europe.

"I believe there is a risk that Elie Wiesel, the Holocaust and other genocides will be forgotten... Elie was a light in the night for the whole world, not just the Jewish one. We should remember him."

We don't yet know if Elie Wiesel will have a lasting legacy. During his life and at the time of his death, Elie Wiesel was the face of the Holocaust victim to the rest of the world. But today, there are already many teenagers who have no idea what happened to the Jews of Europe during the 20th century. Among the younger generations, many people simply have no idea what genocide really is. They do not know how different genocides, not just the Holocaust, have affected and injured the world. Quite often, they are completely unaware that these killings have occurred.

The Holocaust was not solely a Jewish story. Non-Jews were involved in all aspects of it. They were perpetrators of violence and victims of it. They rescued Jews and they persecuted Jews. World War II and the Holocaust had an impact on the entire world. We have to teach about Hitler, the Holocaust and survivors like Elie Wiesel because mass killings and genocides are still happening. Genocides didn't end with the Holocaust.

The nature of human memory is that, in most senses, figures like Elie Wiesel are often gradually forgotten. Most people do not want to think about genocides. They do not want to think about the Holocaust or other mass killings. They are very uncomfortable with the fact that these events happened. So I believe there is a risk that Elie Wiesel, the Holocaust and other genocides will be forgotten. Without a real effort to retain their memory, they may simply disappear from history. Elie Wiesel was a light in the night for the whole world, not just the Jewish one. We should remember him.

Stuart E. Eizenstat

Stuart E. Eizenstat is a lawyer in Washington, DC. He was President Jimmy Carter's Chief Domestic Policy Adviser, and served as United States Ambassador to the European Union and as Special Representative of the President on Holocaust-era issues.

"Elie captured the very best of Judaism. He had an aura of the entire history of the Jewish people from time immemorial. There was a radiance about him."

In 1968, while I was the research director for Hubert Humphrey's presidential campaign, my co-worker Arthur Morse published the book, *Why Six Million Died*. It was the first exposure of what the Roosevelt administration had known about the death of six million Jews. I was shocked. I told myself that if Humphrey wins, I hope I can somehow rectify this tragic aspect of World War II.

Later, when I was chief domestic policy director in the Carter administration, I had the opportunity to help establish a presidential commission to create a Holocaust memorial in Washington, DC. I told President Jimmy Carter that there was only one person with the stature and ability to unify others who could chair the commission—Elie Wiesel.

We reached out to Elie, but initially his reaction both to chairing the commission and to the memorial itself was cool. He wasn't sure it was possible to capture the full horror and lessons of the Holocaust, and second, he didn't feel he should be chairman because he was a scholar, academic, teacher and phi-losopher but not an administrator. It took a number of conversations, but eventually he agreed to chair the commission. That was how we became friends.

Elie's influence was essential to my life. He helped sensitize me to genocides around the world that became very important in terms of Carter's human rights policy and the positions I took during the Clinton administration. It led me to become Ambassador to the European Union and then special envoy on Holocaust issues. With the Cold War over, Eastern Bloc countries needed to restore and restitute synagogues, day schools and cemeteries so Jewish life could be rebuilt. I negotiated $8 billion of Holocaust reparations from Swiss banks, German labor companies and European insurance companies.

To me, Elie embodied the whole suffering of the Jewish people, not just the Holocaust. But he also embodied hope, vision and optimism about the future. He captured the very best of Judaism. He had an aura of the entire history of the Jewish people from time immemorial. There was a radiance about him.

Sonari Glinton

Sonari Glinton is a public radio journalist who covers politics,
business and cars. He was one of NPR's longest-serving
African American male journalists.

"Elie encouraged me to go into journalism. He taught me about taking a stand, speaking directly to people when they do not like it. I still feel that responsibility."

When I was in grade school, I had a really good librarian in my Catholic school on the South Shore of Chicago. I used to joke that the library class was where I learned to be black. I was kind of a lazy kid. I had to do a book report when I was in seventh grade. I went to the bookshelf and literally chose the thinnest book I could find, and it was *Night*. I read it in one night and it punched me in the face.

Elie Wiesel was a big part of why I applied to and chose to attend Boston University. I became a religion major with the idea that I could get into Elie Wiesel's class. I took several of Elie's courses, and they were all great. I still have most of the books on my bookshelf. I remember reading *The Bluest Eye*, a book by Toni Morrison about a dark-skinned girl who longs for blue eyes because they signified "whiteness." When I began my presentation on it in class, and looked down at my notes about skin color, race, blackness, I was overcome. It was a situation I had been in a million times—I was interpreting blackness for white people. I glanced at Elie, who looked at me with encouragement. I immediately began to cry—not a Denzel Washington dignified *Glory* tear, but a full-on Oprah "ugly cry."

He made everyone go to office hours, and there I was a gay black kid trying to find myself in the office of a Jewish Holocaust survivor. For me, it was one of the central moments of my life. I remember apologizing for crying and saying I wanted "to get over it" and get past my feelings about race. I remember Elie said in that voice—he had such a rich voice and his accent was a little like Jackie Mason's, "Why would you want to get over it? It's who you are. This is what makes you special. People needed to see you cry in that class and you needed to cry." He didn't say this in those exact words, but that is what I got out of what he said. I realized that this was the central theme of his work.

Elie gave me the idea that everything about me is a tool to learn and that every hindrance is a plus. Elie encouraged me to go into journalism. He taught me about taking a stand, speaking directly to people when they do not like it. I still feel that responsibility. I was raised in a tradition that you have to stand up even when it makes people feel uncomfortable. That's why I am a journalist. It is about bearing witness.

Martha Hauptman

Martha Hauptman was Elie Wiesel's personal
assistant at Boston University for 27 years.

"I remember Elie's kindness when my mother was dying. He told me to stop coming to the office and instead be with my mother in the hospital. I'll never forget that; nothing was more important to him than my being with my mom."

During the 27 years that I was Elie Wiesel's personal assistant at Boston University, he taught and inspired more than 3,000 students. Not only did he instill a love of learning in them, but in some cases, he changed their lives. There was the student who came out of his office saying that Professor Wiesel had fixed something in her that she did not even know needed fixing, and the student who referred to his office as "sacred space." Many talked about the intensity of the time spent with him, even though it might have been a mere ten minutes. Reinhold Boschki, who came to Boston from Tübingen, is one such student. During his course of study in Germany, someone gave him

Night to read, and he arrived in Boston shortly thereafter to study with the "Master." Since then, his life's work has revolved around the Wiesel oeuvre and teaching the Holocaust to German university students. In 1995, he organized an international conference in Stuttgart, and he is now working on translating all of Elie's work into German.

Elie left a very personal legacy with me. I remember his kindness when my mother was dying. Elie told me to stop coming to the office and that I should instead be with my mother in the hospital. So I was able to be with her during the last weeks of her life. I'll never forget that; nothing was more important to him than my being with my mom.

Annette Insdorf

Annette Insdorf is a film professor at Columbia University. Her books include *Indelible Shadows: Film and the Holocaust* and *Cinematic Overtures: How to Read Opening Scenes.*

> "Elie was a man of action, who bravely traveled to conflict zones, putting his body and reputation on the line in confronting hatred, violence and hypocrisy of all kinds."

I first met Elie Wiesel at a memorial service for Josef Rosensaft, who died in 1975. I was with my mother, Dr. Cecile Insdorf, also a Holocaust survivor; Elie had encouraged her to speak about her experiences, even before the Shoah became part of American cultural parlance.

At the service, it turned out that no microphone was functioning. Because we were standing relatively close to him, I could hear Elie explain that he would not raise his voice. Instead, he spoke eloquently in the soft tones that would characterize every public (and private) talk I ever heard him give: Because he always preferred a whisper to a shout, the listener had to lean in, actively processing his resonant words. Refusing histrionics, he expressed himself with quiet fervor. He inspired me to speak publicly with a similar restraint, never raising my voice or adopting a didactic pose. As the French filmmaker Jean Renoir once proposed, "The more emotional the material, the less emotional the treatment."

When I wrote *Indelible Shadows: Film and the Holocaust* a few years later, I was honored by his positive response and his willingness to write a foreword to the second edition. Although we often disagreed about movies—I tended to defend fiction films about the Shoah while he (understandably) questioned them—we found common ground, especially among foreign motion pictures. In the last years of his life, he trusted my suggestions, and expressed his appreciation for *Ida* from Poland, and *Son of Saul* from Hungary.

His primary translator from French to English was his brilliant, beautiful wife Marion, a cinephile who I first met at the Cannes Film Festival. But occasionally a translation would fall to me, as with his *New York Times* essay about Claude Lanzmann's *Shoah*. Finding the precise interpretation for his thoughts was a privilege as well as a responsibility: Each measured word mattered.

He was not simply a man of letters—a Holocaust survivor who used words to probe the unspeakable. Nor was he simply an educator, who inspired generations of students to think critically about civic responsibility as well as historical memory. He was also a man of action, who bravely traveled to conflict zones around the world, putting his body and reputation on the line in confronting hatred, violence and hypocrisy of all kinds. To me, he was a hero.

I continue to teach courses about film and the Holocaust at Columbia University, always invoking this master of memory. And, true to his inspiration, I do not raise my voice.

Ben Kingsley

Ben Kingsley's Oscar-winning acting career spans more than 50 years and
includes the roles of Otto Frank, Itzhak Stern and Simon Wiesenthal.
In 2018, he played Adolf Eichmann in *Operation Finale.*

"As an actor, being embraced by Elie as a lover of truth and memory released an unstoppable energy in me. When I walk onto a film set, sometimes in a uniform, it is my way of saying, "Boys and girls, I'm telling you, this happened.""

I met Elie Wiesel on several occasions, and we seemed to strike a chord between us. I feel immensely privileged for that. Elie called me a "lover of truth and memory." He put that in writing in a poem and gave it to me. I, in turn, humbly and I hope modestly, said to Elie, "Next time I walk onto a film set that's appropriate for your story, Elie, I will dedicate my performance to you." I needed no further focus, motivation, energy, commitment or passion to get me onto that set every day.

My job is to tell stories, as Elie says in that beautiful poem, "Let us tell tales." It was that mandate from Elie that informed my performance and portrayal of Adolf Eichmann in the film *Operation Finale*. I wanted the world to see the man who had nearly killed Elie, all of his family and six million others and who had done that as a fully conscious adult. None of the people on trial at Nuremberg pleaded insanity. Isn't that extraordinary? Not one of them. So I portrayed Eichman as a man boasting of his accomplishments—as he himself said, "I will leap, laughing, into my grave," boasting of what he had achieved.

And as an actor, being embraced by Elie as a lover of truth and memory, released an unstoppable energy in me. When I walk onto a film set, sometimes in a uniform, it is my way of saying, "Boys and girls, I'm telling you, this happened. It really happened." It is absolutely imperative for this legacy of Elie Wiesel's to continue. It has to, and if it doesn't, it is our loss, and it will be an unfathomable loss.

Ronald S. Lauder

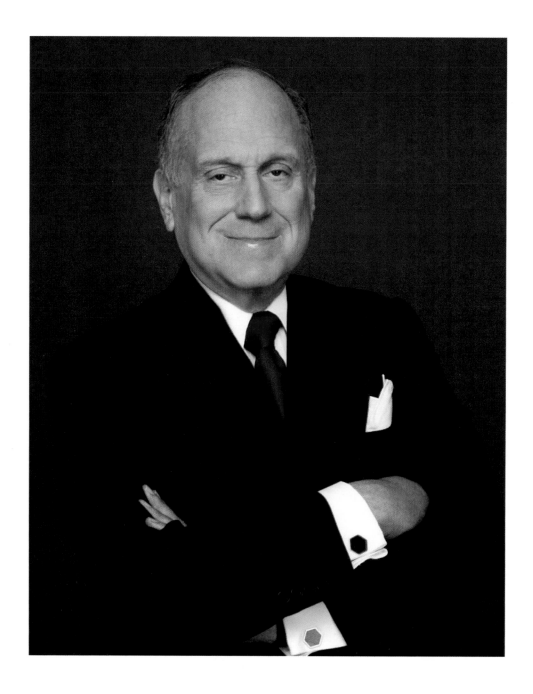

Ronald S. Lauder is President of the World Jewish Congress.
During the Reagan Administration, he was U.S. Ambassador
to Austria and Deputy Assistant Secretary of Defense
for European and NATO policy.

"Elie used his mighty pen to inspire Jews and non-Jews alike to fight hatred and bigotry wherever they fester."

Thirty years ago, I traveled to Auschwitz with Elie Wiesel. I had been to the camp before. I had seen the barbed wire, the barracks, the guard towers. I had stood in the gas chambers where a generation of Jewish children perished at the hands of evil. But to experience Auschwitz through Elie's eyes, through the eyes of the man who taught the world about the horrors of the Holocaust, changed everything for me. It changed the way I think, and it lit a flame in me that burns to this day.

Elie once observed that the survivors of the Shoah "had the right to give up on humanity." But Elie refused to give up. When I joined him at Auschwitz, I found a man not filled with hate, but with sadness and determination. Sadness over all those who were lost, and determination to honor their memory with action and impact.

We talked about the meaning of the Holocaust. And he said something that I will never forget. He told me, "The opposite of love isn't hate. It's indifference." Indifference is what led the world to sit idly by while anti-Semitism in Germany marched on. Indifference made the Holocaust possible.

And so Elie made a commitment: He would never be indifferent to suffering. Through his writing, his activism, and the sheer force of his moral voice, he focused his considerable energies on fighting injustice and evil.

He helped bring the world's attention to the plight of persecuted people in Rwanda and the former Yugoslavia. His book, *The Jews of Silence*, one of his more than 60 works of nonfiction and fiction, raised awareness about Soviet Jewry struggling under the shackles of political oppression. Along with his beloved wife, Marion, herself a Holocaust survivor, he founded the Elie Wiesel Foundation for Humanity. He helped lead the effort to create the U.S. Holocaust Memorial Museum in Washington, DC, bringing the survivor community together to build that enduring institution.

He was a teacher. He not only taught us about the evils of Auschwitz, but about Judaism, about the cause of Zionism, and about the State of Israel, a land he revered and loved. And though he spent his adult life in America, Elie was at home everywhere—in the Old World and the New World, in Yiddish, Hungarian, French, English and Hebrew. He was at ease with world leaders and the many U.S. presidents and world statesmen who sought his counsel.

And he was a writer of uncommon talent. His prose—graceful yet haunting, simple yet forceful—awakened the world to the dangers of indifference. He used his mighty pen to inspire generations—to inspire Jews and non-Jews alike to fight hatred and bigotry wherever they fester.

I am one of those people he inspired. Because of Elie, because of what I learned that day with him in Auschwitz three decades ago, I resolved to speak out whenever I see injustice. It is Elie's example that led me to become involved with the World Jewish Congress, the organization I now have the privilege of leading.

He gave me the courage to speak out on behalf of world Jewry. He inspired me to stand up for Israel, its people, its rights, its security. Everything I do today is because of the example Elie set for me, and for the world.

Elie may have left us, but his memory lives on. As his son Elisha eloquently put it at Elie's funeral service, I still feel his presence inside my heart. We still hear his gentle voice, telling us what he would say to anyone who would listen: that people of good conscience have a moral obligation to speak out, be heard and fight bigotry.

Elie Wiesel was a survivor, a teacher, a Nobel laureate, a scholar and the world's moral compass. But most of all, he was a mensch. May his legacy and wisdom endure as an eternal flame.

Matthew Lazar

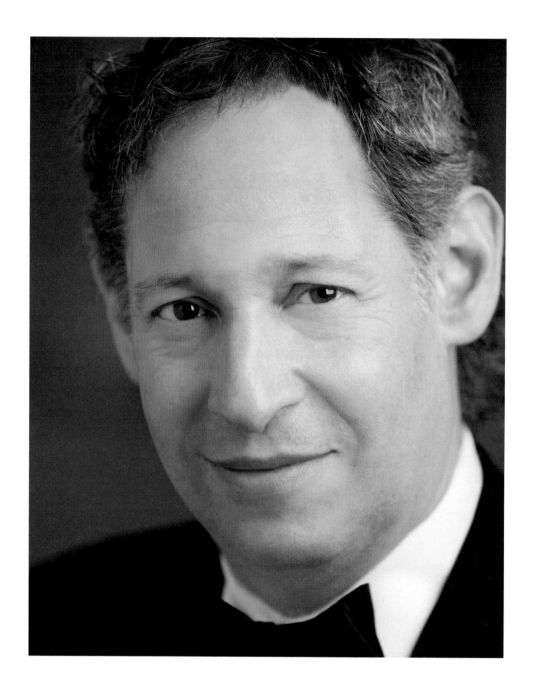

Matthew Lazar is the founder and director of the Zamir Choral Foundation.
He performed with Elie Wiesel in a special concert entitled,
"Memories and Melodies of My Childhood."

> "Hearing Elie singing in joy was a life-changing experience. He was able to express the depth of history and of his soul through music."

Everyone knows about Elie Wiesel's moral and humanistic legacy, but Jewish music was also a small but important part of his essential being. This aspect of his legacy is an unknown gem. Everyone who heard him sing wanted to hear him again and again. He loved music, and his knowledge of it was quite extensive. Hearing him singing in joy was a life-changing experience. He was able to express the depth of history and of his soul through music. Elie remembered singing these songs when he was a child, and I think those memories informed his ability to sing so beautifully.

In 1973, he wrote a play called *Ani Ma'amin: A Song Lost and Found Again*. The title refers to a prosaic rendition of Maimonides's 13-point version of the Jewish principles of faith, and each line begins with the phrase: *Ani ma'amin be-emunah shelemah* ("I believe with perfect faith"). The Zamir Choral that I direct performed a musical version of this with Elie. He once told me: "You can question God, but you cannot be without him." He personified the Jewish experience and was capable of expressing it in a musical voice.

Bernard-Henri Lévy

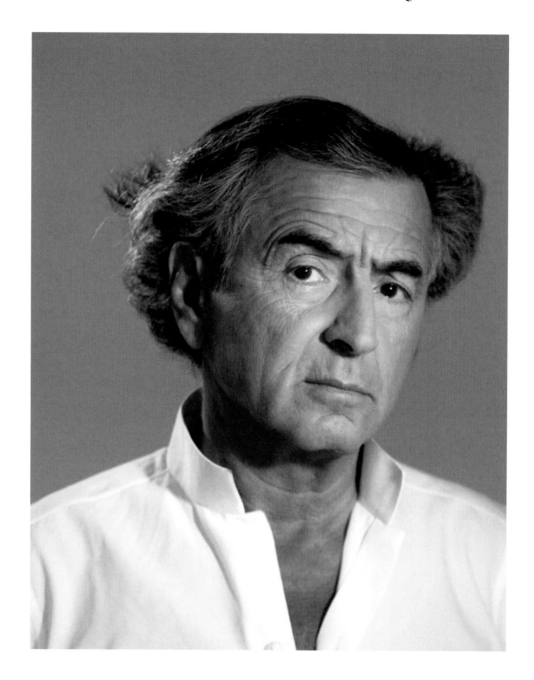

Bernard-Henri Lévy is a French philosopher, documentary filmmaker and author of more than 30 books, including *Left in Dark Times: A Stand Against the New Barbarism.*

> "The greatness of Elie Wiesel, in truth, was to have remained, to the end and under all circumstances, one of those humble Jews who he himself considered to be the crown of humanity."

I do not know if Elie Wiesel was a "great" writer. But I am convinced that he believed that a Jew of his ilk does not come into the world to pursue literature as a profession. His work has neither the inaccessible sublimity of Kafka nor the paradoxically lofty power of Proust—nor, perhaps, the laconic grace of Paul Celan. But he is one of the few to have spoken the unspeakable about the camps. He shares with Primo Levi and Imre Kertész (and how many others?) the terrible privilege of having felt six million shadows pressing against his frail silhouette in an effort to gain their almost imperceptible place in the great book of the dead. Countless lives were reduced to ash and smoke, sloughed into dust or filmy memory—they are lives of which there would have remained, without Wiesel, no name or trace.

His other great virtue, perhaps, is having ensured, through his work and henceforth in the minds of those inspired by that work, that the dark memory of the exception that was the Holocaust will not exclude—indeed, that the Holocaust requires—ardent solidarity with all of the victims of all other genocides.

The greatness of Elie Wiesel, in truth, was to have remained, to the end and under all circumstances, one of those humble Jews who he himself considered to be the crown of humanity.

Joseph Malovany

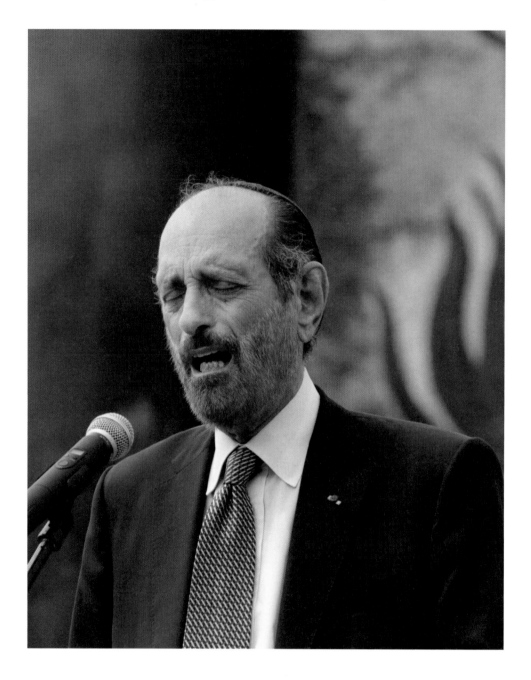

Joseph Malovany is the chief cantor of the Fifth Avenue Synagogue
in New York City. A tenor soloist, he has appeared
at most of the world's major concert halls.

> "I witnessed Elie praying every Shabbat, and unless he was traveling, he obeyed the laws of Shabbat. Despite having a conflicted relationship, spiritually God meant a lot to him. Elie was a man of profound faith and sincerity, committed to Jewish life and the Jewish state."

In the summer of 2016, I conducted Elie Wiesel's funeral. I remember that as we put the casket into the hearse, I kissed it to say good-bye to my friend, Elie. He and I had many conversations about Sighet, his and my mother's hometown in Romania. He described the geography of the town to me; he knew every spot by memory. We called our ongoing conversations the "Sighet connection." I brought back a parchment from the Torah scroll of the local synagogue from one of my trips to Sighet. It still smelled burned, after so many years. When Elie saw that, he broke down and cried bitterly, and I cried with him. It was an unbelievable experience—to sit down and just cry.

People questioned if Elie had faith in God following the Holocaust. I witnessed Elie praying every Shabbat, and unless he was traveling, he obeyed the laws of Shabbat. Despite having a conflicted relationship, spiritually God meant a lot to him. Elie was a man of profound faith and sincerity, committed to Jewish life and the Jewish state.

Elie was extremely musical by nature and talent. He had a beautiful lyric tenor voice—very expressive and very clear. His knowledge of Jewish liturgical music, acquired as a choir member and soloist in the Great Synagogue in Sighet, served him well as a lead singer for more than 30 years at my Fifth Avenue Synagogue. He could chant the haftarah on Shabbat without preparation. He sang Hasidic melodies with full understanding of the text and the music. This legacy will also remain with the Jewish and non-Jewish world for many, many years to come. Everyone should listen to his CD of Hasidic melodies that he loved, most of which he absorbed as a child and a teenager in Sighet.

Elie's legacy is multifaceted. He possessed the unusual quality of being both a teacher and a student. Whenever I saw him, he always had a book in his hands. To whoever was willing to listen, he conveyed the need to read. He believed it was important to learn to enjoy literature and art. He loved to tell other people about what he was reading, but he never instructed anyone to read a particular book. Rather, he spoke about books with love and a keen interest that inspired others to read what he read.

Kati Marton

Kati Marton is a former NPR and ABC News correspondent. Her books include *Enemies of the People: My Family's Journey to America* and *True Believer: Stalin's Last American Spy.*

"When he smiled, the sun seemed to peek through the clouds for just one minute."

Each of us fortunate enough to have known him carries our own Elie in our heart. My friendship with Elie began in a dimly lit Stockholm synagogue in 1981. I arrived from Budapest to attend the first World Conference on Raoul Wallenberg. What good fortune to find myself sharing a pew with Elie! I quickly learned that with him you went to the heart of things fast. A shared language sped our communication. Hungarian was his mother tongue and mine, and French our second language (in his case, the fourth after Hebrew and Yiddish). So, mixing Hungarian and French, I related to Elie what I had just learned in Budapest: that I was not Roman Catholic—the religion I was raised in—but Jewish, and that my grandparents had been part of the same monstrous transport as Elie himself, and with the same destination: Auschwitz. My grandparents did not survive. To this day I have never seen a photograph of them. All this I discovered during an interview with a woman rescued by Wallenberg in Budapest. "How could my parents keep such a basic fact from me?" I asked Elie. I was full of outrage. He was not. Elie gave his characteristic shrug and that look of his: angelic sadness. "Your parents survived," he said. "You are here because of that fact—don't be so tough on them."

Elie was not a stranger to any human frailty. What had he not seen during his long night in that cauldron of cruelty? Nor did it bother him that I was ignorant of his faith and its rich culture and history—now suddenly my inheritance. "You are a good person," he said, and that seemed sufficient for us to be friends—for three decades.

Much later, I told him that I had met a still-spry lady in her 80s—my grandparents' fellow passenger on the death train, who told me that my grandmother, Anna, recited the Shema—the Jewish prayer which begins "Hear, O Israel"—the whole way to Auschwitz. "So," Elie said, "You have the faith in your bloodstream." Nothing about his fellow man surprised Elie. People are not angels—this he knew. During a long drive back to New York from my son's New England boarding school, Elie told me Bernard Madoff had robbed him of his savings. "A Jew!" I spluttered, "A Jew could do this to you!" He shook his head. "*Un escroc,*" he said simply. A crook, in French. Again, the small shrug as if to say, Jews have crooks, too.

There was something paradoxical to me about a deeply observant Jew who was at the same time very much a man of the world. But that did not mean he forgave or rationalized cruelty or inhumanity—whoever its victims. Cambodians, Bosnian Muslims, Tibetans, Syrians—he spoke up for all of them until the last. Nor was he surprised that the world had once again turned demented and glacial (his words). Nor that again we find sound reasons to stay on the sidelines while inhumanity unfolds before our eyes in real time in Syria.

How we miss his strict moral authority, his simple, powerful, searing words. "Mr. President," he told President Ronald Reagan, who planned on laying a wreath near Nazi graves, buried under snow in Bitberg Cemetery, "this place is not your place!"

I loved Elie Wiesel's handsome, lined, infinitely sad face. It was the face of Central Europe, my father's face. When he smiled, the sun seemed to peek through the clouds for just one minute. To say that we shall not see his like again is to state the obvious. Far more meaningful would be if we could say of the atrocities Elie witnessed as a child—we shall not see their like ever again. If only we could.

Chaim Peri

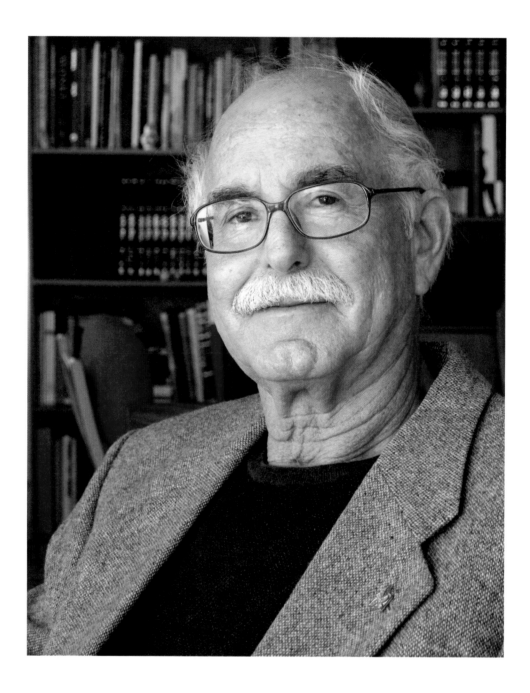

Chaim Peri was the director of Israel's Yemin Orde Youth Village, a home and school that serves at-risk and disadvantaged teenagers from around the world.

"I will never forget the elation I felt that moment, hearing Elie saying the Kaddish for Tzipora, his voice blending with children's squeals of joy and merry music sounding from outside. Is there any better, or more tangible, affirmation of Jewish continuity?"

The Elie imprinted in my heart is an Elie of joy. Our connection came about thanks to his wife Marion's devotion to Ethiopian children in Israel. Marion's working for this cause with her whole being meant the world to Elie. He derived immense joy from her being at center stage, with him offering support from behind the scenes. Together, as a unit, they emitted an aura of softness and perfect reciprocity. Yet it was an active partnership, built of vision, spirit and the determination to handle any and all obstacles, including the most trifling bureaucracies. To me, Marion's efforts had much more to them than meets the eye. I could tell that both she and Elie regarded the ingathering of this long-lost African Jewish tribe as the bright antipode to the darkest of the dark, the radiance of daytime following our people's nightmarish past.

When Marion established first-rate culture and learning centers in Israel, warm havens for Ethiopian children, they were named Beit Tzipora, the Home of Tzipora, for Elie's little sister, who died in Auschwitz. It signaled the inclusion of the Ethiopian-Jewish cause in their most intimate circle. This was to be a home of happiness, of joie de vivre, of the life that Tzipora Wiesel never had. I vividly recall the festive opening of Beit Tzipora in Ashkelon. Elie stepped to a side room to join a minyan of young Ethiopians for the mincha prayer. I will never forget the elation I felt that moment, hearing Elie saying the Kaddish for Tzipora, his voice blending with children's squeals of joy and merry music sounding from outside. Is there any better, or more tangible, affirmation of Jewish continuity?

Itzhak Perlman

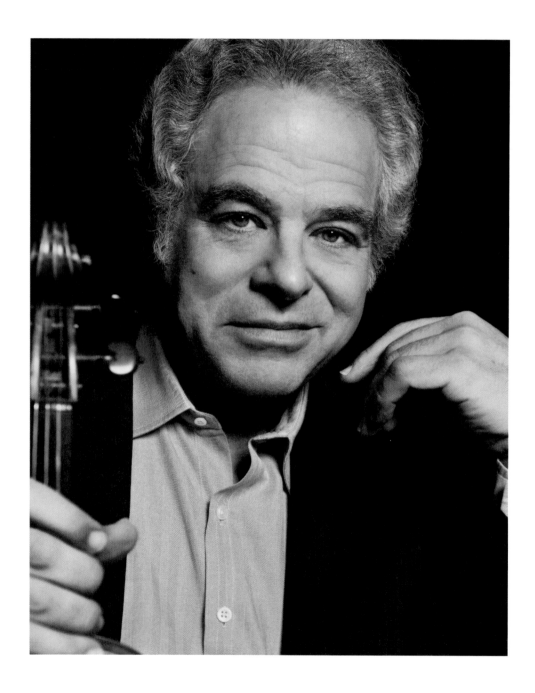

Itzhak Perlman is a Grammy and Emmy Award-
winning violinist and conductor.

"Elie was the Jewish people's spokesperson.
Elie looked after our moral landscape and paid
attention to what happened to Jews around the world.
We needed a person like that.
We needed a person to look out for us."

If I were to explain to young people why they should study Elie Wiesel's work, I would tell them that Elie is the Jewish people's spokesperson. Elie looked after our moral landscape and paid attention to what happened to Jews around the world. We needed a person like that. We needed a person to look out for us. The fact that he was accepted by heads of state was extremely important, because when Elie spoke, people listened. Also, he was a wonderful scholar. I loved to go to his lectures at the 92nd Street Y. He was fascinating.

One of the great experiences that I had with Elie, believe it or not, was of him singing. On Yom Kippur, at one of the synagogues in New York City, he would sing the first prayer. It was so touching. I always looked forward to hearing him sing. Because of his background, it was not just someone singing, but rather someone singing from the heart, someone singing from his personal experiences and from a viewpoint of history. That's what he was about, he was about Jewish history and remembering what had happened. Music is an international language, I am not surprised that Elie would burst out in a *nigun* to express what he was really feeling.

We have to continue to talk about the Holocaust; we cannot just assume it will be remembered. The Holocaust must be remembered, and it must be associated with the Jews. Elie Wiesel was our spokesperson to make sure we didn't forget it. Now he has passed the torch to all of us; we must not forget what happened.

Mark Podwal

Mark Podwal is an artist who illustrated some of Elie Wiesel's books.
He is also a dermatologist on the faculty of the New
York University School of Medicine.

> "Elie said many times, that our Jewish tradition says that we must speak truth to power. I think that's one of his main legacies—giving voice to the truth no matter what."

Elie Wiesel's most important legacy was bringing real awareness of the Holocaust to the public consciousness. The great turning point for his work came during a speech he made in a White House ceremony in 1985, when he received the Congressional Gold Medal of Achievement from President Ronald Reagan. Reagan was about to visit a military cemetery in Bitburg, Germany, where some Nazi SS guards were buried. There was a great uproar about Reagan's proposed visit, and people wondered what Elie Wiesel would say about it. When press attention started to build before the ceremony, the White House made efforts to contain the situation. There were attempts to limit the scope and content of Elie's speech, and they moved the ceremony to a much smaller room. Even though I had designed the medal Elie was receiving, I, along with many others, was no longer able to attend the event.

Elie was not quelled, and in his speech that day he called on Ronald Reagan to cancel the visit, famously saying, "That place, Mr. President, is not your place. Your place is with the victims of the SS." NBC carried the speech live, and the next day it was quoted in headlines in all the major newspapers. Before that speech, many people had not read *Night*, and they really didn't know who Elie Wiesel was. Elie said that day, and many times afterwards, that our Jewish tradition says that we must speak truth to power. I think that's one of his main legacies—giving voice to the truth no matter what.

People have often remarked to me that Elie Wiesel always looked pained, and asked if he enjoyed life and if he ever laughed. Elie had a wonderful sense of humor and appreciated a good joke, but I can't publicly repeat the best jokes he made! He always made time for his friends. Elie held my son at his circumcision and gave the sermon at his bar mitzvah. And he was very thoughtful and sensitive. When my mother died, Elie consoled me, saying, "Death is the price of life." At Elie's funeral, his son, Elisha, eulogized him by saying that Elie finally has the opportunity to ask God all the difficult questions. Knowing him, I am sure Elie will question God's answers.

Dina Porat

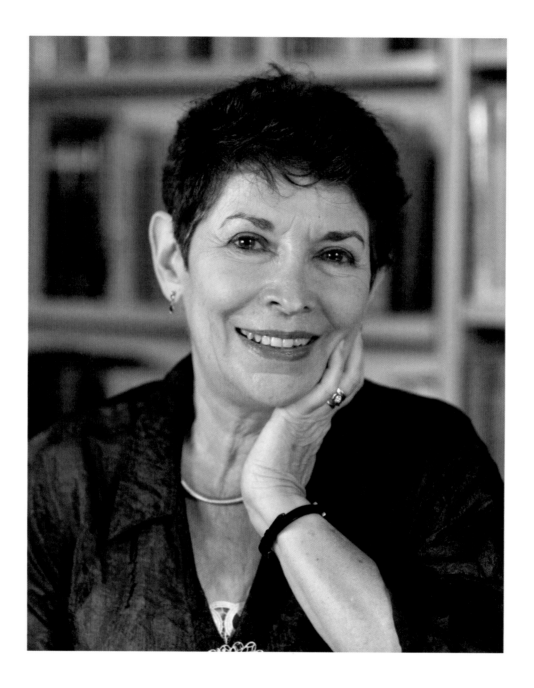

Dina Porat is the chief historian at Yad Vashem and the head of the Kantor Center for the Study of Contemporary European Jewry at Tel Aviv University.

"He was a champion of human rights, in many cases in situations that didn't relate to the Jewish people. He fought for human rights in Mongolia, Rwanda, South Africa, for Kurds and for Armenians."

Elie Wiesel's main legacy is that one should study and learn about the Holocaust as a starting point for understanding minority rights, relations between different groups and democracy. He did not believe one should study and remember the Holocaust just for its own sake or only for the sake of the Jewish people. Rather, we should understand the Holocaust to improve the world. In particular, young people should think about evils of the past and then work to fix the world. He was a champion of human rights, in many cases in situations that didn't relate to the Jewish people. He fought for human rights in Mongolia, Rwanda, South Africa, for Kurds and for Armenians. He was extraordinarily active in whatever was happening at a given time that related to human rights and human suffering.

His legacy, in certain ways, is a complicated one. Critics, here in Israel as well as elsewhere, have said that although he spoke out about human rights in so many places, he never criticized Israel or any of its policies and actions. He was often asked why he never spoke out about human rights violations in Israel. He said that since he did not live in Israel and was not a citizen of Israel, he did not have the right to criticize Israel. He stood unconditionally by Israel's side. This stance is difficult to reconcile with his fighting so passionately for the rights of suffering people in so many different parts of the world. I think he saw the complexity of the Palestinian situation and how it was being politicized in parts of the world, and he did not want to be part of that.

Jean Bloch Rosensaft

Jean Bloch Rosensaft is Assistant Vice President for Communications and Public Affairs at Hebrew Union College-Jewish Institute of Religion. She is also director of HUC-JIR's Heller Museum.

"Elie inspired me to stand guard against all manifestations of Holocaust denial, exploitation and immoral equivalence."

My sister Gloria and I were four and eight years old, respectively, when we first met Elie Wiesel. It was 1960 and we were aboard the SS Jerusalem, adventurously exploring remote corners of the ship's deck. Occasionally, we would encounter a solitary, melancholy man, who would appear like an apparition in the distance. One evening as we were strolling with our parents, he approached us from afar. Imagine our surprise when my father Sam Bloch exclaimed "Elie!" and rushed forward to embrace him. Elie's reserved countenance lifted into a warm smile as we were introduced. Later, my father explained that Elie was his good friend and a very important writer. As a young girl and avid reader aspiring to be a writer one day, this immediately made an impression.

Throughout my childhood during the 1960s, my father's close relationship with Elie filtered into my life in powerful ways. *Night*, my first literary introduction to the Shoah, substantiated my survivor parents' stories at a time the Holocaust was neither taught nor memorialized in the broader Jewish community. Reading *The Jews of Silence* motivated my own teenage activism on behalf of Soviet Jewry. Elie's passionate advocacy for Israel resonated with my own Zionist commitment from an early age on. When we children were included in the Bergen-Belsen survivors' annual April 15th celebration of their day of liberation, convened by my future father-in-law Josef Rosensaft, Elie was always with us. As Elie rose in prominence, we all took enormous pride in the fact that he was the preeminent "voice" of the survivors as they emerged to take their rightful place as significant public figures.

Beginning in the late 1970s, Elie encouraged me and other leaders of the second generation to mobilize a movement that would sustain our parents' legacy into the future. His presence at our second-generation conferences elevated the scope of our agenda and energized us. He appointed a group of us to serve as advisors to the U.S. Holocaust Memorial Council, so that our generation would have an active, constructive presence at board meetings and on committees. He was our staunch ally when our Second Generation Advisory Committee worked with the U.S. Holocaust Memorial Museum (USHMM) to conceive and organize "Life Reborn" in 2000. This international conference and exhibition brought to light the heretofore little-known liminal years of the DP camps, where many of our generation were born as the survivors ceased to be victims and created new families and vibrant, autonomous communities.

Despite the preponderance of male survivor leaders a generation ago, Elie prized the voices of women survivors, and he valued egalitarianism. He encouraged my mother to tell the story of how a righteous Gentile farmer hid her, her parents and her aunt for over two years, thus saving their lives. He valued my mother-in-law Hadassah Rosensaft's prominent role in President Carter's Commission on the Holocaust, the U.S. Holocaust Memorial Council, and the creation of the USHMM. And Elie's confidence in his wife, Marion, as his translator and full partner in his extraordinary public life modeled a unique synergetic union that galvanized his career and greatly broadened his impact. Personally, Elie inspired me to stand guard against all manifestations of Holocaust denial, exploitation, and immoral equivalence. I will continue to carry his message of tolerance, peace and hope into the future.

Top: Elie, Israeli Prime Minister Golda Meir and Josef Rosensaft in Jerusalem at a 1970 commemoration of the 25th anniversary of the liberation of Bergen-Belsen. **Bottom left:** Sam Bloch, Elie and Prime Minister Itzhak Rabin at the 30th anniversary of Bergen-Belsen liberation. **Bottom right:** Elie with U.S. Ambassador to the UN, Arthur Goldberg. **Opposite page:** Elie (seen here with his wife Marion) officiated at Jean Bloch's and Menachem Rosensaft's wedding.

Menachem Z. Rosensaft

Menachem Z. Rosensaft is General Counsel at the World Jewish Congress and teaches about the law of genocide at the law schools of Columbia and Cornell Universities.

> "Elie retained and exuded a love for humankind. He did not allow himself to succumb to hatred or to retreat into an insular mindset."

Elie Wiesel was a towering intellectual figure whose writings, thoughts and actions fundamentally changed the mindset of his and following generations. More than anyone else, he imposed an uncompromising yet comprehensible awareness of the Shoah and its moral implications onto a global society that had long avoided confronting it. He wrote and spoke in psalmic terminology, *min hameitzar*—out of the depths.

As I write, a series of photographs returns to my mind: It is August 1979 and members of President Carter's Commission on the Holocaust are visiting Auschwitz-Birkenau. Five survivors of the death camp hold on to one another, Elie in the middle, Dr. Hadassah Rosensaft—my mother—and Sigmund Strochlitz on either side of him, and Chris Lerman and Mannes Schwarz beside them. Elie is there not only as chairman of the commission but as the linchpin of a close-knit collective who had emerged from the inferno, and who wordlessly gave each other strength.

I was privileged to be Elie's first teaching assistant after his appointment as distinguished professor of Judaic studies at New York's City College in 1972. I vividly remember his attentiveness to his students' questions, regardless of whether they had anything to do with the subject at hand. But he also imparted wisdom in a way his students would not forget. At the end of our first year there, he gave the commencement address, speaking about the many obstacles Holocaust survivors had overcome. "What can we learn from their experience?" he asked. "First, that it is given to man to build upon ruins, to invent hope when there is none, to call upon love and faith in a world that lacks both. Second, that suffering gives man no privileges; it all depends on what he does with it. If he uses his suffering against man, he betrays it; if he uses it to fight evil and human-

ize destiny, then he elevates it and elevates himself."

The first aspect of Elie's legacy is to ensure that the memory of the Shoah, both of its victims and its survivors, becomes ingrained in the consciousness of humankind. In large part thanks to Elie, the Shoah is no longer viewed in abstract, impersonal terms. As a result of his writings and teachings, the perspective of the victims has become essential to the way we understand the Holocaust.

A second, equally important aspect of his legacy is a refusal to allow the Holocaust to be universalized, diluted or trivialized. For a long time, there were efforts to minimize the Jewish essence of the genocide and to ignore that it was the culmination of thousands of years of anti-Semitism. The Shoah was viewed by many as just another war-related atrocity. But six million Jews were murdered exclusively because they were Jews—not because they were Poles or Hungarians, not because of their political views or sexual orientation, but because they were Jews. That was an absolute line in the sand for him. At the same time, Elie insisted that the lessons of the Shoah must be seen as universal. What he taught was that the identity of the victims of a genocide—any genocide—is essential to giving the event the dignity of proper remembrance. He made clear that the primary lesson to be drawn from the Holocaust is the need to fight against all forms of bigotry, xenophobia and hatred, and that silence is never an option.

The last major aspect of his legacy is his refusal to allow his experiences during the Shoah to dehumanize or embitter him. He retained and exuded a love for his family, for his friends and for humankind as a whole. He did not allow himself to succumb to hatred or to retreat into an insular mindset. His approach to his readers and his audiences was always one of hope—one that provided light rather than darkness.

Kali Rubaii

Kali Rubaii is a Mellon postdoctoral research fellow in the Humanities Research Center at Rice University. She is the cofounder of the Islah Reparations Project.

"Elie's legacy forces contemplation. He offers us moral ambiguity, and I can work with that. Elie Wiesel inspired me to write and to work on behalf of Palestinians."

In 2004, I won a high school essay contest about applying the lessons of *Night* to a contemporary issue, employing Elie Wiesel's argument that the Holocaust, while unique, had universal implications. I wrote about enjoying the luxuries of American consumerism during the onset of the U.S. invasion of Iraq. I appeared on *The Oprah Winfrey Show* with other winners and with Elie himself. He was lovely, grandfatherly, warm—exactly who you would expect him to be.

I was disheartened when I later learned of some of his positions on the Palestinians and, over time, I saw that he made exceptions to his own lessons. He called the Goldstone Report, which examined allegations of [Israeli] war crimes during the Gaza War, a "crime against the Jewish people." I was surprised; was this not the kind of witness-bearing Elie so eloquently promoted? Elie Wiesel's ability to articulate the Holocaust, to imbue people with the obligation to bear the weight of memory, was powerful and important. But his political contradictions challenge us to accept that ideas can be bigger than their proponents. We don't have to be paralyzed by the precondition of moral perfection to lend our support or to be inspired. Elie's legacy forces contemplation. He offers us moral ambiguity, and I can work with that. Elie Wiesel inspired me to write and to work on behalf of Palestinians. His voice, to me, is a voice for their human rights—even if he couldn't see it.

Daniel B. Shapiro

Daniel B. Shapiro is a Distinguished Visiting Fellow at the Institute for National Security Studies in Tel Aviv. He was U.S. Ambassador to Israel and Senior Director for the Middle East and North Africa in the Obama Administration.

"Elie taught us about Jewish identity and Jewish pride, and also about the importance of being engaged in the world."

In my mind, Elie Wiesel's lasting legacy will be defined by four lessons:

First, the Shoah cannot be explained; rather, it must be grappled with. The Holocaust is almost unfathomable, given its scale, its brutality and its devastating impact on the Jewish people—and on humanity more broadly.

Just as Elie struggled for 70 years to understand how the Holocaust was allowed to unfold, how one could believe in God in its aftermath, and how we could fail to prevent future genocides, we all must grapple with these questions.

Second, Elie left behind a tremendous legacy in terms of his Jewish identity and his deep and abiding sense of Jewish peoplehood. Born in Romania, imprisoned by the Nazis, a Holocaust refugee who moved from Europe to Israel to America, Elie lived in many countries, but his Jewish identity never wavered. He was Jewish through and through, and yet he also managed to be a full and active member of American and international civil society. Elie taught us about Jewish identity and Jewish pride, and also about the importance of being engaged in the world.

Third, Elie taught us about the critical role of remembrance and our collective responsibility in this regard. He was a leading force behind the establishment of the United States Holocaust Memorial Museum. Elie was the museum's founding chairman and remained deeply involved for more than three decades.

Fourth, Elie taught us all to speak truth to power. As I was just becoming politically aware, his public stance on President Reagan's visit to the cemetery in Bitburg was a model for how to express dissent in an open society.

In Israel, Elie Wiesel is widely admired. He represents resilience, perseverance and the indomitable Jewish spirit. He also represents personal tragedy, and this is something every Israeli feels.

In some sense—in a collective sense—Israel is a nation founded by survivors and refugees from persecution and political violence. Israelis could thus relate his personal story to their own national narrative. His story, like Israel's, is a story of survival against impossible odds.

Natan Sharansky

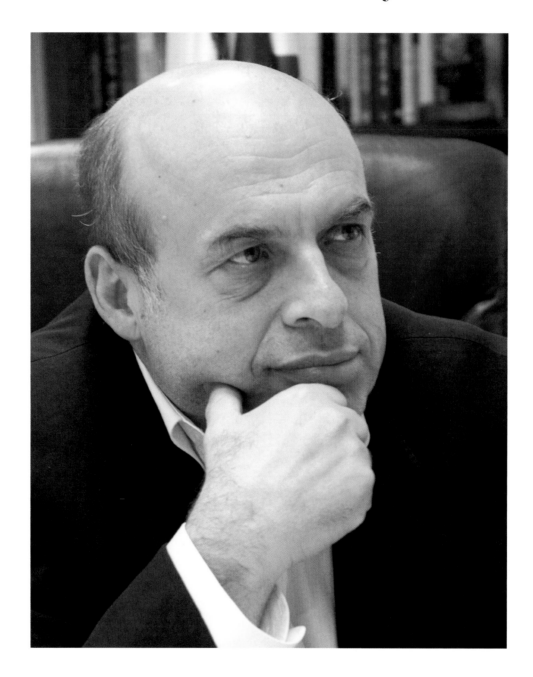

Natan Sharansky spent nearly a decade in Soviet prisons as a refusenik and has served in ministerial positions in several Israeli governments. He recently stepped down as chairman of the Jewish Agency for Israel.

"Elie Wiesel wanted to be remembered for his work for Soviet Jewry as much as for the Holocaust. He viewed this work as a sign of what we Jews could do if we worked together."

Elie Wiesel was a warrior against the destructive power of silence. He understood the obligation to speak out and, in all ways, to have a loud and active voice. He was the first to break the silence about the struggles of Soviet Jews. By writing *The Jews of Silence* (1966), he prevented world Jewry from remaining silent. He showed Jews that they had a choice. They could remain passive and quietly leave things just as they were, or they could speak out against what was happening to Soviet Jews.

He himself had a strong and loud moral voice. He was part of the collective movement for change as well as a leader in it. He was a great sage for the Jewish community, but he was also very much a part of the community. He wanted to be remembered for his work for Soviet Jewry as much as for the Holocaust. He viewed this work as a sign of what we Jews could do if we worked together. He felt deeply connected both to the roots of the struggle and to its success.

Elie Wiesel was very polite, very correct and very intelligent. He felt the responsibility of history on his shoulders. He was a mixture of a Jewish professor and a *hazan* (cantor). He could speak in a very deep and philosophical way on any Jewish topic. Regardless of how famous he became, he continued to study and teach. He had a very sentimental connection to Yiddish. He wanted the Yiddish language to survive and thrive and was concerned that younger people should study it. On *erev* Shabbat, another side—the *hazan*—would come out, and he would stop everything and sing Jewish melodies. He sang beautifully; it was very moving to listen to him. Whenever we were together on *erev* Shabbat, I would ask him to sing. Politically and personally, his voice reminded us of our past and taught us to always use our voices to build our future.

Kathleen Kennedy Townsend

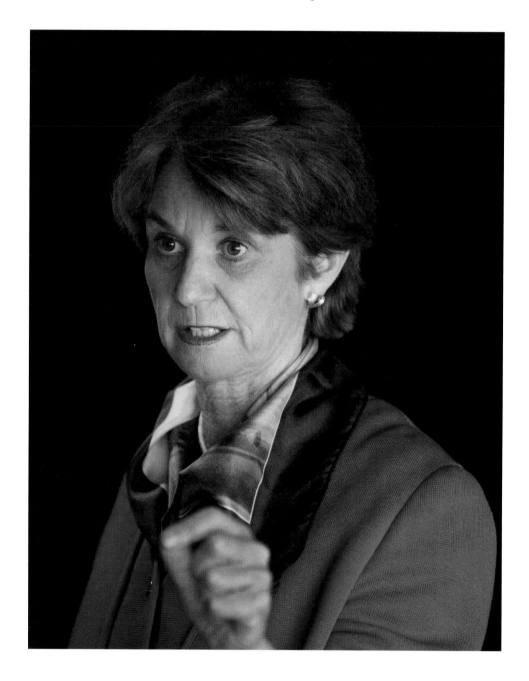

Kathleen Kennedy Townsend is Director of Retirement Security at the Economic Policy Institute and Founder of the Center for Retirement Security at Georgetown University. She was Maryland's first woman lieutenant governor.

> "There was something burning inside of Elie, a flame ignited by injustice and pain. He was willing to share that part of himself. Pain can make people retreat from life, but it opened Elie to the world."

I met Elie Wiesel through the Robert F. Kennedy Foundation. The foundation created a human rights award in 1984, and Elie was our hero because he spoke so eloquently about what happened during the Holocaust. We had first heard of human rights from Eleanor Roosevelt, but there was a new interest in the topic during the 1980s as we learned about human rights violations such as people being tortured, imprisoned and murdered from Elie Wiesel. Although he first made his mark with his book on the Holocaust, he became a voice for all those suffering human rights abuses around the globe. Because of Elie's prominence and wisdom, his voice made a real difference. The most important thing I've learned through human rights work is that the worst thing that can happen to a victim is to feel alone and deserted. When someone like Elie Wiesel pointed the world's conscience towards these victims, it gave them the ability to go on and to have hope.

His biggest legacy is ensuring that people know there was a Holocaust and that we should remember it. *Night* has been read by millions of people around the world. That book made it impossible to hide the Holocaust. And once someone with his eloquence chose to write about it, many others then wrote books about what had happened. He inspired people to want to know the truth. For example, a friend of mine discovered some letters with swastikas on them when his father died. He read *Night* and then found the courage to have the letters translated. It turned out that his father had left Germany in 1939, and these were the letters his family had sent to him after he left the country. Elie created an audience that hadn't existed, one that was willing to listen to and discover these stories.

Elie not only spoke eloquently; he was able to listen carefully to other people's stories. There was something burning inside of him, a flame ignited by injustice and pain. He was willing to share that part of himself. Pain can make people retreat from life, but it opened Elie to the world. It was because of him that people could listen to what had happened. He made that his mission. Just because people have had pain, doesn't mean they can create. Creation is done out of love. Elie Wiesel never lost his ability to love.

Oprah Winfrey

Oprah Winfrey is a media executive, television producer, actress and talk show host. She is best known for *The Oprah Winfrey Show.*

> "Elie is my hero not only for what he endured, but for what he became — a teacher, a sage, an activist, a humanitarian, a great spirit. Despite the horrors he survived, he was one of the most loving spirits I have ever known."

Elie Wiesel was a hero to me, a mentor and a friend; and that's not a word I use lightly, "friend." He was a true friend. Being in his presence, exposed to his wisdom, has been one of the great blessings of my life. He is my hero not only for what he endured, but for what he became—a teacher, a sage, an activist, a humanitarian, a great spirit. Despite the horrors he survived, he was one of the most loving spirits I have ever known. Wiesel lived through a dark, dark night where everyone was there either to kill or to die.

Evil is never the end of the story; the end of the story is still ours to write. Wiesel taught us that we must not forget; that there is no greater sin than that of silence and indifference. In doing so he has not just illumined the past, he has illumined the future. For he himself embodies the only adequate response to evil, a heart that cares so deeply about human suffering—and responds to it so passionately—that evil itself will one day be conquered by a love so great.

With Elie Wiesel, you knew you were in the presence of someone who had endured the unimaginable worst of times and could still give and teach the best that love has to offer. Every day he taught, lectured and lived compassion, peace, empathy for other souls and truth.

Ruth Wisse

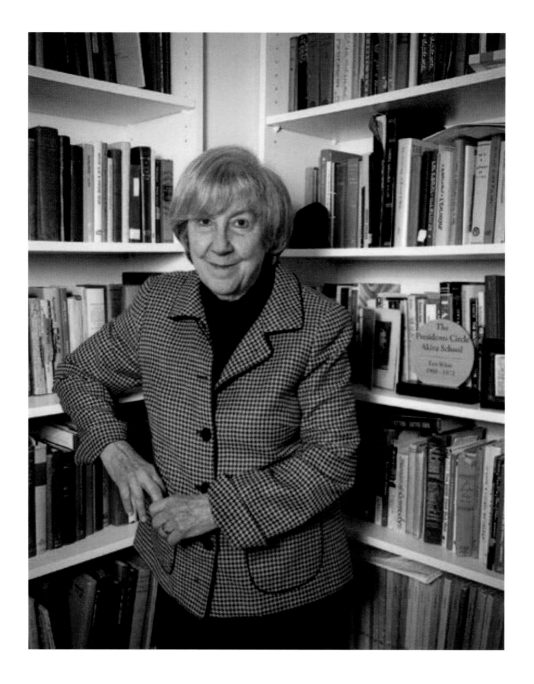

Ruth Wisse is professor of Yiddish literature and comparative literature at Harvard University. Her books include *No Joke: Making Jewish Humor* and *Jews and Power*.

"Elie wanted to be a part of and contribute to the world around him. Yiddish literary critics used to call this 'being more than a writer.'"

Elie Wiesel was less an icon to me than a polyglot journalist and writer with a strong Jewish background and easy writing style. What I most appreciated about him when compared to a number of his friends and fellow survivors such as Piotr Rawicz and Jerzy Kosinski was his resistance to the suicidal eddy that sucked them in. Unlike them and others—Primo Levi and Jean Amery and Paul Celan—he seemed to draw appreciation of life from being a member of the Jewish people. Whatever doubts he registered about divine intervention, he remained a synagogue goer. He was a passionate lover of Israel, who did not yield to the literary fashion of signing anti-Israel petitions. He looked for the chance to speak Yiddish with a fellow Jew, and it was in that capacity that I got to know him. The several times I had the pleasure of meeting with him we spoke Yiddish about Yiddish writers we knew.

I confess that I liked the first, angry, vengeful Yiddish version of his memoir *Un di velt hot geshvign—And the World Was Silent*—more than the existentialist-oriented French and English versions of *Night*. His strengths and limitations as a writer seem to me to be one and the same—he wrote for his audience, and adapted his stories to the expectations of his readers. This was not pandering, as it is for writers of pulp fiction, but rather a professional's ability to adjust his register linguistically and culturally to the given audience. The same skill made him a gifted teacher, a powerful speaker and public figure. He wanted to be a part of and contribute to the world around him. Yiddish literary critics used to call this "being more than a writer."

May his memory be a blessing.

Peter Wittig

Peter Wittig is Germany's Ambassador to the United Kingdom. Previously, he was Ambassador to the United States and Permanent Representative to the United Nations. He twice served as President of the United Nations Security Council.

> "Elie Wiesel believed not in the collective guilt of the German people, but in a special responsibility and the mutual and ongoing need to remember this painful chapter of German history—to draw lessons from the past."

I had the honor of meeting Elie Wiesel and his wife in New York, where I was Ambassador to the United Nations. He was being presented with the highest Order of Merit of the Federal Republic of Germany. After a moving ceremony, we sat next to each other at lunch. I was immediately captivated by the charm and the quiet, natural charisma of this handsome man with melancholic eyes. We talked about his work as a teacher and professor at Boston University, which he seemed to have enjoyed tremendously. It so happened that my son—a high school senior—had just returned from a visit to Auschwitz and had tasked me with asking Elie Wiesel to autograph his copy of *Night* for him. Elie complied with a wonderful personal dedication—a treasure that we all still cherish.

Elie Wiesel was a courageous fighter for peace, human dignity and reconciliation. His legacy has shaped the German culture of remembrance forever. He was courageous despite having experienced one of the darkest chapters in the history of mankind.

Elie Wiesel survived the death camps of Auschwitz and Buchenwald, after having been deported by the Nazis at the age of 15. For ten years after his liberation in 1945, he refused to write about the cruelties he experienced during the Holocaust. He only broke his self-imposed silence in the early 1950s, when he published a haunting memoir about his personal experiences in the concentration camps. It laid the foundation for his unremitting dedication to Holocaust remembrance.

From then on, Elie Wiesel became one of the most powerful and charismatic voices against forgetting, a great messenger to mankind. He kept speaking about the unspoken, about uncomfortable truths and against suppressed memories. During his ongoing fight for remembrance, he found particularly clear and unequivocal words for the German people. One of his greatest contributions is that he stressed the enduring responsibility of the German people regarding their own history. In doing so, he significantly influenced how German post-war generations—including my own—deal with the legacy of the Holocaust and the heavy burden of its lasting aftermath.

In the year 2000, half a century after his liberation from Buchenwald, Elie Wiesel gave a moving speech before the German parliament, not as a prosecutor, but as a witness, as the world's conscience. His admonishing words particularly resonated at a time when German Holocaust remembrance was undergoing a major shift through the passing away of eye witnesses and the rise of a younger generation inclined to look beyond the atrocities of the past. At this pivotal point, his powerful plea not to turn away or to neglect their immense continuing responsibility struck a chord, especially with those who had not personally witnessed the Nazi atrocities.

Elie Wiesel believed not in the collective guilt of the German people, but in a special responsibility and the mutual and ongoing need to remember this painful chapter of German history—to draw lessons from the past and to fight against any atrocities committed against mankind around the world.

One of his greatest contributions is his encouragement of future generations to relentlessly and courageously fight for the truth and to promote ongoing remembrance. His legacy will last forever, and the German people as a whole as well as me personally are deeply indebted to him.

Elisha Wiesel

INTERVIEW

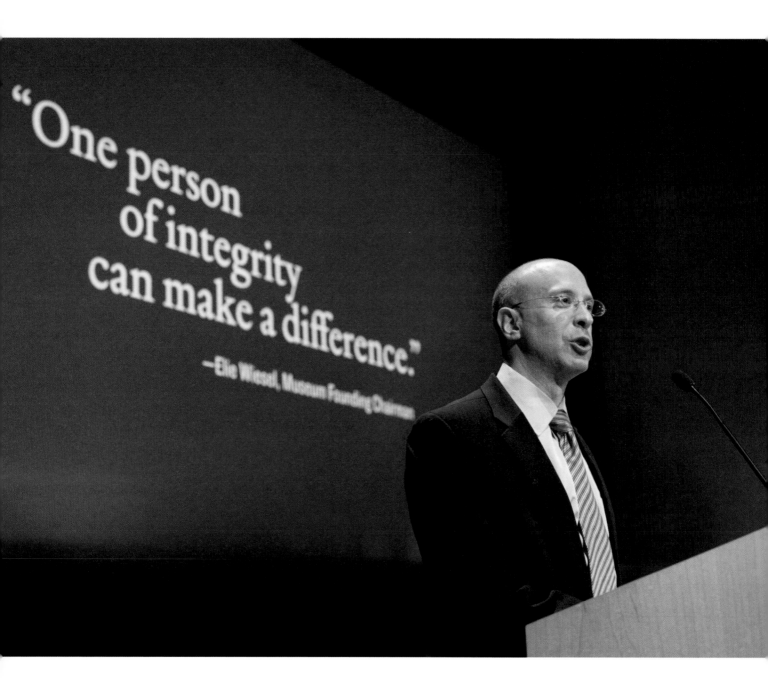

Elisha Wiesel is the son of Elie and Marion Wiesel.

> "I can pick up a book from my bedside and I can hear him speak. I think that is true in a larger sense as well as in terms of his legacy."

What are some of your early memories of your dad? We had a summer home in Amagansett. I was probably three or four years old when we went there, and I remember him singing me Russian army songs. And I remember him trying to rescue a bird that had fallen out of a tree. I dragged him away from his desk where he was working because a little bird had fallen out of a tree. I got him to pay attention to the bird and help it.

What was he like as a dad? We're familiar with his public persona; what can you tell us about his more private side? My dad had an enormous amount of confidence in me, even though at times it might have seemed somewhat misplaced for where I was in life. He really only had two rules for me growing up. One he gave me early, and one he gave me later. The rule he gave me earlier was that my wife was to be Jewish (whether through birth or conversion he didn't care). That was really the only ground rule I had with him for the first few decades of my life. I could do what I wanted and explore different things. I remember I came home from college with a purple mohawk my freshman year, and my dad was not fazed. He said, "I love you, and I would walk down the street with you any time, anywhere. I am not embarrassed. I would take you to shul like this and out to dinner. I love you. You are my son. You can do anything you want as long as you marry Jewish." That was the major constraint. He was a good dad. I think that confidence he had in me, and that unconditional love, had a very good long-term effect.

The second rule was that he wanted me to say Kaddish for him every day after he passed, which I did. Those were the only two substantial things he asked me to do for him.

You've kept both of your promises to your father. How have you gained from keeping those commitments?

I understand now that if I had not married within the faith, experiences that I currently derive tremendous meaning from would be missing. For instance, the connection that I had to my father was not just that of a father and son, it happened in a very Jewish context. When I said Kaddish for him for 11 months, I was not just connecting with him. I felt connected with his forebears as well. I had a real sense of history, going back thousands of years, of what it meant to be part of a lineage with certain traditions, rituals and values. For almost 2,000 years, when a parent has passed, the Jewish child has said Kaddish. There is something profound about that. As I prepare my own son for his bar mitzvah and watch my daughter learning Hebrew, despite this crazy modern life with all of its distractions, I have this same sense of history and continuity. I think about where I came from, where I am and where my Jewish children will go in the future. That's deeply meaningful and very grounding.

Did your relationship to Judaism change as a result of saying Kaddish for your father? I used to give my dad a hard time about the time he spent in shul. I used to say, "It's the same prayers over and over again. Do you really think someone is listening? Wouldn't it be more interesting to hear a new speech or read a new book?" I really couldn't understand why someone would voluntarily want to spend their time in shul. I'm sure my father had a lot he could have said to me, but what he chose to say was that prayer and being in shul made him feel closer to his father. That is certainly something I now understand.

Are there any other memories about your dad you would like to share with our readers? I helped convince him to toss out the first pitch at a World Series game. The commissioner of baseball, Peter Ueberroth,

called him in 1986 to ask him to throw out the first pitch. Originally when he got the message, my father was pretty scared. He wondered why he was getting a call from a commissioner, a word that had all sorts of military overtones for him and made him think of occupation. Finally he was persuaded to return the call even though he thought it was a mistake—what could they want with him that had to do with baseball? Then there was an issue that he couldn't throw because it was still Sukkot, a Jewish holy day. But I told him he had to do it! We realized that if they had a car come for him, they could pick him up after sundown, just in time to throw out the first pitch. He did it and it was a really big deal for me even though I was a Yankees fan, not a Mets fan.

There are different cute stories along those lines, ones about my dad finding his way in the modern world. He knew the names of the staff on the Concorde by their first names, and they all knew him

be? He wanted to be thought of as a good Jew. That was the only standard by which he measured himself. In most conversations, it wasn't about which president he met or any of that—all of which was meaningful to him; he valued that he had grown to play a role on the world stage. But he looked at himself as his mother and father and grandparents would have evaluated him. That was always in his mind, what would they think of him and his life and what he had made of it. For him, the guiding principle that governed that lens was always, "Have I been a good Jew?" That meant many different things to him. If you unpacked what a good Jew was, it meant being a good human being and a good father; a leader in the community when leadership was needed; a good husband; someone who respected and brought respect to the memory and traditions and name of his ancestors; someone who was humbled by the concept of man's place in the universe but still felt mandated to fix the world; and someone who, when approached by

"My dad said: 'You are my son. You can do anything you want as long as you marry Jewish.'"

when it still used to fly. But on the other hand, he couldn't pump gas for his car, and he was amazed when friends like Ted Koppel could!

There's another story about a friend and me in seventh grade when we were studying for a test. We were playing soccer outside, and my father kept saying that we needed to come inside and study for our test. We said no. So he said, "If I take on both of you in soccer and I score a goal, will you go study for your test?" This came from a man who had probably never kicked a ball before in his life, so we said yes. As soon as we agreed, he turned into this super-amazing soccer athlete who was dancing rings around us and scoring goals—just to get us to go inside and study for the test. I don't remember how I did on the test, though!

What did your father want his legacy to the world to

people, would make time to talk with them and make them feel welcomed and listened to.

What is his legacy to the world? The actions he took, the speeches he made and the words he wrote. In him, we had such an exceptional person share the planet with us. The good news is that we don't have to guess at his legacy. He left his words behind, and, in most cases, they are unambiguous. For people who want to know what my father thought, they don't have to ponder it and wonder what my father would have said. He was a prolific writer, and he wrote about many different circumstances with moral significance.

As I mourn him, I realize that I am not like other mourners because whenever I want to hear my father's voice, I can pick up a book from my bedside and I can hear him speak. I think that is true in a larg-

er sense as well in terms of his legacy. If people want to know what my father thought of something, they should read his books and reread his speeches. It is all there. If I had to pick one word about his legacy it would be "available." His legacy is readily available to anyone who wants to know it.

When I had to pick a profession (and only one profession) to give the funeral home immediately after his passing, I chose "teacher," as I think that is who he was in the broadest sense. But he also remembered journalism as his first and earliest profession, and it was one that he remained deeply invested in.

What did your father see as the most significant challenge facing Jews today? Intermarriage was at the top of the list. He saw intermarriage and assimilation as very significant threats to the Jewish people. He always felt he was at a crux because he was at the end of a line. It was his job to continue it and to make sure that he was not the last. He felt a connection to the fact that for thousands of years, Jews had been transmitting information down the generations in a certain way with certain values. I think he was very concerned that the line would end with him.

If you were speaking to a young person, particularly to someone who had not had the opportunity to meet or hear a Holocaust survivor, about why they should read your father's work, what would you say? This is a hard question. In the 1930s and 1940s, there were many Jews who said, "I don't practice, I don't observe, I don't affiliate. Why should I read books by Jewish authors? Why should I care about Jewish history?"

When the enemy came, they didn't care whether you were a Jew who ate shrimp and lobster on Saturday morning or if you were a Jew who had payot and a black hat. If you are Jewish, this is part of your story and it is where you come from. If you are human, this is now part of your story and where you come from.

Do you think there is any risk of your father being forgotten? For thousands of years, the Jewish people have faithfully transcribed the works and thoughts and identities of those who have contributed to the intellectual and spiritual learnings of the people. I am confident that for thousands of years to come, my father has earned his place in that community.

In His Own Words

Essays, Speeches, Interviews

Remembering

ESSAY | MOMENT MAGAZINE | MAY/JUNE ISSUE 1975

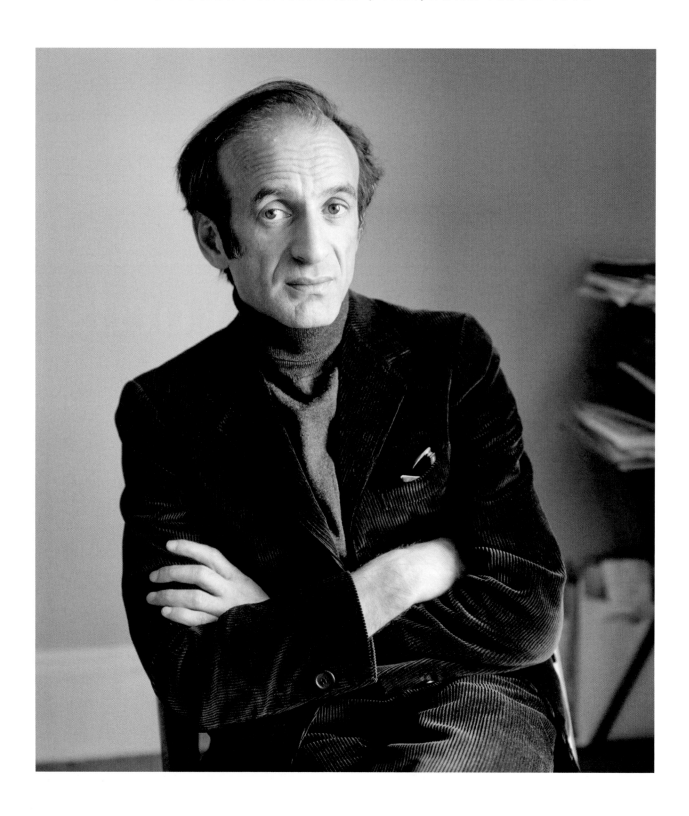

REMEMBERING

ELIE WIESEL

Let us remember, let us remember. For that is all we can do for those young boys and girls who, on a sunny April day, 32 years ago, rose in the Warsaw ghetto and made a desperate last bid to live — or at least die — as free human beings.

They were few. Most of the ghetto population of 500,000 had already vanished into the death factories of Treblinka. Only some forty thousand were still alive.

Let us remember all of them — all the six million. Those who took up arms and fought but also those who did not, those who had the strength to resist but also those who chose to die in silence. For even the heroes perished as victims and even the victims were heroes.

The Warsaw ghetto was but a symbol. What happened there, happened everywhere. There were other Jews, in other ghettoes. They all shared the same fate. All were condemned by the executioner not for what they had done but for what they were: Jews. Old and young, rich and poor, scholars and workers, beggars and dreamers, sages and artists—all were marked. And they were so many that they could people an entire kingdom which, indeed, they did. Theirs was the Kingdom of Night.

Forgotten by mankind, forsaken by God, they lived alone, suffered alone, fought alone. Alone they faced mighty legions — among the mightiest of all time. Alone — that is the key word, the haunting theme. Alone—with no allies, no friends. Totally, desperately alone.

Every underground movement received financial help and military assistance from special headquarters set up in London. Only the Jewish resistance organization received nothing. Its members were the loneliest and saddest soldiers of the war.

And they knew it. Read their appeals, their letters. Read the Ringelblum archives, miraculously preserved. The ghetto fighters, most of them in their early twenties and some of them in their teens, lived and died with no illusions; they knew that for the outside world they were expendable.

Their pleas — to the Allies and their leaders, to the free world and its conscience, to the Jews and their heart — leave one shivering. A single air-drop, a single rescue attempt would have shown them that their struggle and their sacrifices were not in vain and that people — even if they could not effectively help — at least cared. But nobody cared.

It was April and the mood was festive in the sunny streets of Warsaw. Enjoying the spring weather, many strollers went to watch the burning ghetto: the most exciting spectacle in town. All over the world, Christians celebrated Easter and Jews observed Passover with song and prayer — as always. People attended theaters, concerts, movie premières; not one dinner party was cancelled. Uninformed? No: three days after the start of the uprising, reports about it were published in the New York *Times* and in every major American newspaper. Detailed accounts: the German onslaught, the fierce Jewish resistance, the step by step annihilation of the largest ghetto in Europe. It was all there. In print. People had but to read. They paid no attention. Warsaw was too far. And the victims were Jews. And anyway, the priorities were elsewhere. Roosevelt was busy fighting the war and so was Churchill. Everybody was too busy to remember the handful of Jewish warriors who had turned every house in the ghetto into a fortress. Unbelievable but true: the German attack against the Warsaw ghetto lasted longer than the initial invasion of sovereign Poland, with its armies and resources.

That the German leadership was concerned and even worried, has been ascertained. A frantic Governor General Hans Frank discussed the uprising with his military staff at an emergency meeting which had originally been scheduled to plan Hitler's birthday celebrations. Goebbels noted in his diary that the Führer was extremely disturbed by the Jewish rebellion and that he had asked to be kept constantly advised of its developments. Now we realize, wrote Goebbels, what we could expect from Jews if they were armed.

Unfortunately the impact was not as strong on the outside world. On April 26, as the insurrection entered its second week, Mordechai Anielewicz, the young Commander-in-Chief of the most extraordinary army in Jewish history, wrote a letter to a friend — Yitzchak Zuckerman (Antek) — on the Aryan side, a letter filled with prophetic anger:

"... For a week we have been involved in a life and death struggle. Our losses are enormous, our end is imminent ... But while we are in possession of arms, we shall continue to resist. We have rejected the German ultimatum to capitulate because the enemy knows no pity and we have no choice ... As we feel our last days approaching, we ask you to remember how we have been betrayed."

Yes—they were betrayed. The world knew and kept silent. In those days and nights of destiny, the solitude of the Jewish people was matched only by God's. We let them down. We let them suffer alone, fight alone. And yet, and yet. They did not die alone — not quite — for something of all of us died with them. ✦

Congressional Gold Medal of Achievement

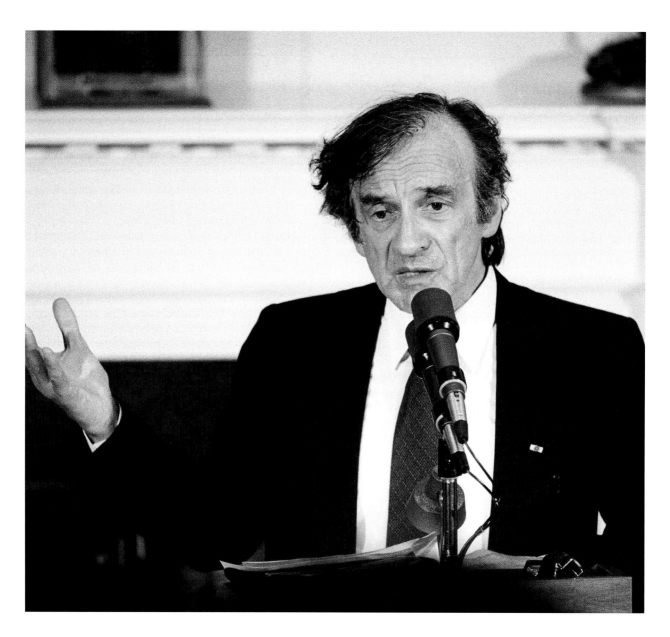

Mr. President, Mr. Vice President, Secretary Bennett, Mr. Agresto, Mr. Regan, very distinguished members of the Senate, my friends—and of the House:

Mr. President, speaking of reconciliation, I was very pleased that we met before so a stage of reconciliation has been set in motion between us. But then we were never on two sides; we were on the same side. We were always on the side of justice, always on the side of memory, against the SS, and against what they represent.

It was good talking to you, and I'm grateful to

you for the medal. But this medal is not mine alone. It belongs to all those who remember what SS killers have done to their victims. It was given to me by the American people for my writings, teaching, and for my testimony.

When I write, I feel my invisible teachers standing over my shoulders, reading my words and judging their veracity. And while I feel responsible for the living, I feel equally responsible to the dead. Their memory dwells in my memory.

Forty years ago, a young man awoke, and he found himself an orphan in an orphaned world. What have I learned in the last 40 years—small things. I learned the perils of language and those of silence. I learned that in extreme situations when human lives and dignity are at stake, neutrality is a sin. It helps the killers not the victims. I learned the meaning of solitude, Mr. President.

my entire life reciting their names, I would die before finishing the task. Mr. President, I have seen children—I have seen them being thrown in the flames alive. Words—they die on my lips.

So, I have learned. I have learned, I have learned the fragility of the human condition. And I'm reminded of a great moral essayist, the gentle and forceful Abe Rosenthal, having visited Auschwitz once wrote an extraordinary reportage about the persecution of Jews, and he called it, "Forgive them not Father, for they knew what they did."

I have learned that the Holocaust was a unique and uniquely Jewish event, albeit with universal implications. Not all victims were Jews, but all Jews were victims. I have learned the danger of indifference, the crime of indifference. For the opposite of love, I have learned, is not hate but indifference. Jews were killed by the enemy but be-

> "I have learned the danger of indifference, the crime of indifference. For the opposite of love, I have learned, is not hate but indifference."

We were alone, desperately alone. Today is April 19, and April 19, 1943, the Warsaw Ghetto rose in arms against the onslaught of the Nazis. They were so few and so young and so helpless, and nobody came to their help. And they had to fight what was then the mightiest legion in Europe. Every underground received help, except the Jewish underground. And yet, they managed to fight and resist and push back those Nazis and their accomplices for six weeks.

And yet, the leaders of the free world, Mr. President, knew everything and did so little or nothing or at least nothing specifically to save Jewish children from death.

You spoke of Jewish children, Mr. President; one million Jewish children perished. If I spent

trayed by their so-called allies who found political reasons to justify their indifference or passivity.

But I've also learned that suffering confers no privileges. It all depends what one does with it. And this is why survivors of whom you spoke, Mr. President, have tried to teach their contemporaries how to build on ruins, how to invent hope in a world that offers none, how to proclaim faith to a generation that has seen it shamed and mutilated. And I believe, we believe, that memory is the answer—perhaps the only answer.

A few days ago on the anniversary of the liberation of Buchenwald, all of us Americans watched with dismay and anger as the Soviet Union and East Germany distorted both past and present history. Mr. President, I was there; I was there

when American liberators arrived, and they gave us back our lives. And what I felt for them then nourishes me to the end of my days, and will do so. If you only knew what we tried to do with them then, we who were so weak that we couldn't carry our own lives—we tried to carry them in triumph!

Mr. President, we are grateful to the American Army for liberating us. We are grateful to this country—the greatest democracy in the world, the freest nation in the world, the moral nation, the authority in the world. And we are grateful especially to this country for having offered haven and refuge and grateful to its leadership for being so friendly to Israel.

Mr. President, do you know that the Ambassador of Israel, who sits next to you, who is my friend and has been for so many years, is himself a survivor? And if you knew all the causes we fought together for the last 30 years, you could be prouder of him. And we are proud of him.

And we are grateful, of course, to Israel; we are eternally grateful to Israel for existing. We needed Israel in 1948 as we need it now. And we are grateful to Congress for its continuous philosophy of humanism and compassion for the underprivileged.

And as for yourself, Mr. President, we are so grateful to you for being a friend of the Jewish people, for trying to help the oppressed Jews in the Soviet Union and to do whatever we can to save Sharansky and Abe Stolyar and Iosif Begun and Sakharov and all the dissidents who need freedom. And of course, we thank you for your support of the Jewish State of Israel.

But, Mr. President, I wouldn't be the person I am, and you wouldn't respect me for what I am, if I were not to tell you also of the sadness that is in my heart for what happened during the last week. And I am sure that you, too, are sad for the same reasons. What can I do? I belong to a traumatized generation. And to us, as to you, symbols are important. And furthermore, following our ancient tradition—and we are speaking about Jewish heritage—our tradition commands us, quote: "to speak truth to power."

So may I speak to you, Mr. President, with respect and admiration, of the events that happened. We have met four or five times, and each time I came away enriched, for I know of your commitment to humanity. And, therefore, I am convinced, as you have told us earlier when we spoke that you were not aware of the presence of SS graves in the Bitburg cemetery. Of course, you didn't know. But now we all are aware. May I, Mr. President, if it's possible at all, implore you to do something else, to find a way, to find another way, another site. That place, Mr. President, is not your place. Your place is with the victims of the SS.

Oh, we know there are political and strategic reasons, but this issue, as all issues related to that awesome event, transcends politics and diplomacy. The issue here is not politics but good and evil. And we must never confuse them, for I have seen the SS at work, and I have seen their victims. They were my friends. They were my parents. Mr. President, there was a degree of suffering and loneliness in the concentration camps that defies imagination. Cut off from the world with no refuge anywhere; sons watched helplessly their fathers being beaten to death; mothers watched their children die of hunger. And then there was Mengele and his selections, terror, fear, isolation, torture, gas chambers, flames—flames rising to the heavens.

But, Mr. President, I know and I understand, we all do, that you seek reconciliation. So do I. So do we. And I, too, wish to attain true reconciliation with the German people. I do not believe in collective guilt, nor in collective responsibility; only the killers were guilty. Their sons and daughters are not. And I believe, Mr. President, that we can and we must work together with them and with all people. And we must work to bring peace and understanding to a tormented world that, as you know, is still awaiting redemption.

I thank you, Mr. President.

TMC6005

CONFIRMATION COPY OF TELEPHONED MESSAGE VIA RCA

 TOT5801 JJH700600 6745300WWW
URNX CO URDB 134 6745300WWW
NEWYORKNY 134/133 15 1516

HONORABLE RONALD REAGAN, PRESIDENT OF THE
UNITED STATES
WASHINGTON DC

AT AN EMERGENCY MEETING OF THE UNITED STATES HOLOCAUST
MEMORIAL COUNCIL TODAY, UNANIMOUS APPROVAL WAS GIVEN TO
ME TO TRANSMIT TO YOU OUR DEEP ANGUISH OVER THE CURRENT
PLANS FOR YOUR TRIP TO GERMANY NEXT MONTH TO SEEK AN
URGENT PERSONAL MEETING WITH YOU TO REVIEW THE SITUATION
AND HOPEFULLY TO MODIFY YOUR PLANS.
IT IS PRECISELY BECAUSE YOU HAVE SO IMPRESSED US IN THE
PAST WITH YOUR DPPE UNDERSTANDING OF THE NEED TO KEEP
MEANING AND THE MEMORY OF THE HOLOCAUST ALIVE THAT WE HAVE
BEEN SO KEENLY DISTURBED BY YOUR PLANS.
THE COUNCIL HAS POSTPONED FURTHER ACTIONS UNTILL I CAN REPORT
BACK TO THEM LATER THISWEEK ON CHANGES WHICH MAY BE MADE IN
PLANS.
 ELIE WIESEL, CHAIRMAN, U.S. HOLOCAUST MEMORIAL COUNCIL

COL REAGAN, TODAY, PLANS. PLANS. PLANS. WIESEL, CHAIRMAN, U.S.

HEBREW UNION COLLEGER
1 WEST 4TH STREET
NEWYORK NY10012

Photo: Letter that Elie sent President Ronald Reagan to express the United States Holocaust Memorial Council's "deep anguish" over the president's plans to visit Bitburg Cemetery in Germany.

Nobel Peace Prize Acceptance

SPEECH | OSLO, NORWAY | DECEMBER 10, 1986

It is with a profound sense of humility that I accept the honor you have chosen to bestow upon me. I know: Your choice transcends me. This both frightens and pleases me.

It frightens me because I wonder: Do I have the right to represent the multitudes who have perished? Do I have the right to accept this great honor on their behalf? … I do not. That would be presumptuous. No one may speak for the dead, no one may interpret their mutilated dreams and visions.

It pleases me because I may say that this honor belongs to all the survivors and their children, and through us, to the Jewish people with whose destiny I have always identified.

I remember: It happened yesterday or eternities ago. A young Jewish boy discovered the kingdom of night. I remember his bewilderment, I remember his anguish. It all happened so fast. The ghetto. The deportation. The sealed cattle car. The fiery altar upon which the history of our people and the future of mankind were meant to be sacrificed.

I remember: He asked his father: "Can this be true?" This is the 20th century, not the Middle Ages. Who would allow such crimes to be committed? How could the world remain silent?

And now the boy is turning to me: "Tell me," he asks. "What have you done with my future? What have you done with your life?"

And I tell him that I have tried. That I have tried to keep memory alive, that I have tried to fight those who would forget. Because if we forget, we are guilty, we are accomplices.

And then I explained to him how naive we were, that the world did know and remained silent. And that is why I swore never to be silent whenever and wherever human beings endure suffering and humiliation. We must always take sides. Neutrality helps the oppressor, never the victim. Silence encourages the tormentor, never the tormented. Sometimes we must interfere. When human lives are endangered, when human dignity is in jeopardy, national borders and sensitivities become irrelevant. Wherever men or women are persecuted because of their race, religion or political views, that place must—at that moment—become the center of the universe.

Of course, since I am a Jew profoundly rooted in are the Palestinians to whose plight I am sensitive but whose methods I deplore. Violence and terrorism are not the answer. Something must be done about their suffering, and soon. I trust Israel, for I have faith in the Jewish people. Let Israel be given a chance, let hatred and danger be removed from her horizons, and there will be peace in and around the Holy Land.

Yes, I have faith. Faith in God and even in His creation. Without it no action would be possible. And action is the only remedy to indifference: the most insidious danger of all. Isn't this the meaning of Alfred Nobel's legacy? Wasn't his fear of war a shield against war?

There is much to be done, there is much that can be done. One person—a Raoul Wallenberg, an Albert Schweitzer, one person of integrity, can make a difference, a difference of life and death. As long as one dissident is in prison, our freedom will not be true. As long as one child is hungry, our lives will be filled with

"No one is as capable of gratitude as one who has emerged from the kingdom of night. We know that every moment is a moment of grace, every hour an offering..."

my people's memory and tradition, my first response is to Jewish fears, Jewish needs, Jewish crises. For I belong to a traumatized generation, one that experienced the abandonment and solitude of our people. It would be unnatural for me not to make Jewish priorities my own: Israel, Soviet Jewry, Jews in Arab lands... But there are others as important to me. Apartheid is, in my view, as abhorrent as anti-Semitism. To me, Andrei Sakharov's isolation is as much of a disgrace as Josef Biegun's imprisonment. As is the denial of Solidarity and its leader Lech Walesa's right to dissent. And Nelson Mandela's interminable imprisonment.

There is so much injustice and suffering crying out for our attention: victims of hunger, of racism, and political persecution, writers and poets, prisoners in so many lands governed by the Left and by the Right. Human rights are being violated on every continent. More people are oppressed than free. And then, too, there anguish and shame. What all these victims need above all is to know that they are not alone; that we are not forgetting them, that when their voices are stifled we shall lend them ours, that while their freedom depends on ours, the quality of our freedom depends on theirs.

This is what I say to the young Jewish boy wondering what I have done with his years. It is in his name that I speak to you and that I express to you my deepest gratitude. No one is as capable of gratitude as one who has emerged from the kingdom of night. We know that every moment is a moment of grace, every hour an offering; not to share them would mean to betray them. Our lives no longer belong to us alone; they belong to all those who need us desperately.

Thank you, Chairman Aarvik. Thank you, members of the Nobel Committee. Thank you, people of Norway, for declaring on this singular occasion that our survival has meaning for mankind.

A Jewish Plea for Bosnian Children

ESSAY | MOMENT MAGAZINE | OCTOBER, 1993

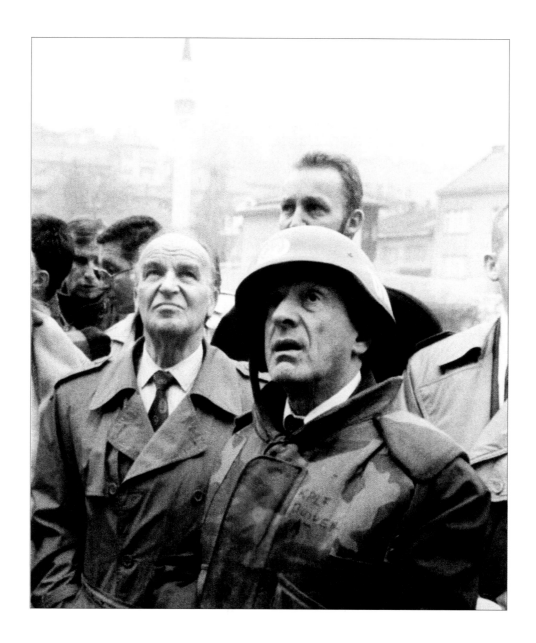

My appeal to President Clinton at the inaugura-tion of the Holocaust museum to do something, anything, to stop the violence and death in Saraje-vo, brought me voluminous correspondence. On the whole favorable, if not enthusiastic, it also in-cluded a few discordant reactions.

Did I act properly? More generally, should a Jew be concerned by the atrocities committed in Bos-nia? Jew that I am, must I prove sensitive only to what happens to Jews? I have no wish to impose my views on others, but I feel it is incumbent upon me to clarify my position.

Having lived what I have lived, having written what I have written, I consider all Jewish priorities my own priorities; but they are not exclusive. In other words: Israel's needs, the threats hanging over her, the urgent demands of the Diaspora regarding Jewish education—it is the duty of every Jew aware of his or her condition to respond to these. A Jew defines himself by his relationship to the community of Israel. To be indifferent to its fate is to distance and detach oneself. But a Jew detached is a Jew assimilated, and therefore lost.

That said, I can understand that a Jew might declare himself free of any obligation toward what is not Jewish, but I would like him to understand that I do not agree with him. If the distress of human beings, whatever their religious or ethnic affiliation leaves me indifferent, by what right can I reproach author of a book that insults Jewish memory.

Of whom am I a defender? Of the victims. More particularly, of the children. As so often happens everywhere, adults make war and children die. How can a Jew like me not denounce such an outrage? Now and then people ask me, what can we do? Being an expert in neither military strategy nor political science, I don't know the answer. Press our leaders in Washington? Urge them to act more firmly and resolutely? Demand a more serious response on the part of the United Nations? As always, my questions are worth more than my answers, all the more so as I have no real answers.

I have only the oppressive feeling that on another continent men are killing, women are raped, children lay dying, while for the rest of the world, life goes on. I do not compare, I would never compare,

> "I would never compare the situation in Bosnia or anywhere else to what we so inadequately call the Holocaust; but I know that there is a link between them, as there is among all events. The world that yesterday accepted too easily the systematic annihilation of six million Jews is today consenting to the brutal and cruel damnation that strikes orphaned children and mothers in mourning in Bosnia."

others for their passivity toward suffering Jews?

Certainly the war in the former Yugoslavia presents no specifically Jewish aspect. In Belgrade I met Jews who called themselves Serbian patriots, while in Sarajevo I found Jews who were defending the Bosnia cause. I know nothing about the state of mind of Jews in Croatia, but I do know that in their place I would mistrust their president. Despite what his Jewish and non-Jewish defenders say, Franjo Tudjman [the former president of Croatia who wrote *Wastelands*] cannot be a friend of the Jewish people—he who is the the situation in Bosnia or anywhere else to what we so inadequately call the Holocaust; but I know that there is a link between them, as there is among all events. The world that yesterday accepted too easily the systematic annihilation of six million Jews is today consenting to the brutal and cruel damnation that strikes orphaned children and mothers in mourning in Bosnia. Let us remember them in these days of judgment. Let us remember that on Rosh Hashanah the Jew crowns God, not only sovereign of the Jewish people, but king of the entire universe.

Photo: Elie and Bosnian President Ali Ja Izetbegovic looked at war-torn ruins in the old part of Sarajevo, Bosnia and Herzegovina in November 1992.

50th Anniversary of the Liberation of Auschwitz

SPEECH | AUSCHWITZ, POLAND | JANUARY 27, 1995

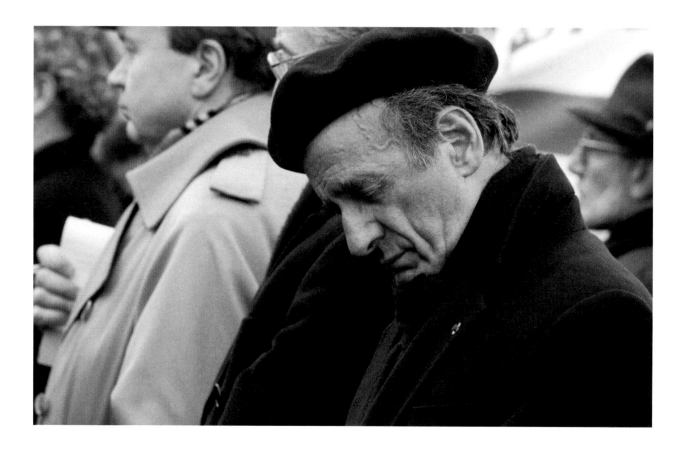

"After Auschwitz, the human condition is not the same, nothing will be the same."

Here heaven and earth are on fire.

I speak to you as a man, who 50 years and nine days ago had no name, no hope, no future and was known only by his number, A7713.

I speak as a Jew who has seen what humanity has done to itself by trying to exterminate an entire people and inflict suffering and humiliation and death on so many others.

In this place of darkness and malediction we can but stand in awe and remember its stateless, faceless and nameless victims. Close your eyes and look: Endless nocturnal processions are converging here, and here it is always night. Here heaven and earth are on fire.

Close your eyes and listen. Listen to the silent screams of terrified mothers, the prayers of anguished old men and women. Listen to the tears of children, Jewish children, a beautiful little girl among them, with golden hair, whose vulnerable tenderness has never left me. Look and listen as they quietly walk towards dark flames so gigantic that the planet itself seemed in danger.

All these men and women and children came from everywhere, a gathering of exiles drawn by death.

Yitgadal veyitkadash, Shmay Rabba.

In this kingdom of darkness there were many people. People who came from all the occupied lands of Europe. And then there were the Gypsies and the Poles and the Czechs... It is true that not all the victims were Jews. But all the Jews were victims.

Now, as then, we ask the question of all questions: what was the meaning of what was so routinely going on in this kingdom of eternal night. What kind of demented mind could have invented this system?

And it worked. The killers killed, the victims died and the world was the world and everything else was going on, life as usual. In the towns nearby, what happened? In the lands nearby, what happened? Life was going on where God's creation was condemned to blasphemy by their killers and their accomplices.

Yitgadal veyitkadash, Shmay Rabba.

Turning point or watershed, Birkenau produced a mutation on a cosmic scale, affecting man's dreams and endeavors. After Auschwitz, the human condition is no longer the same. After Auschwitz, nothing will ever be the same.

Yitgadal veyitkadash, Shmay Rabba.

As we remember the solitude and the pain of its victims, let us declare this day marks our commitment to commemorate their death, not to celebrate our own victory over death.

As we reflect upon the past, we must address ourselves to the present and the future. In the name of all that is sacred in memory, let us stop the bloodshed in Bosnia, Rwanda and Chechnia; the vicious and ruthless terror attacks against Jews in the Holy Land. Let us reject and oppose more effectively religious fanaticism and racial hate.

Where else can we say to the world, "Remember the morality of the human condition," if not here?

For the sake of our children, we must remember Birkenau, so that it does not become their future.

Yitgadal veyitkadash, Shmay Rabba: Weep for Thy children whose death was not mourned then: Weep for them, our Father in heaven, for they were deprived of their right to be buried, for heaven itself became their cemetery.

The Perils of Indifference

SPEECH | THE WHITE HOUSE | APRIL 12, 1999

Mr. President, Mrs. Clinton, members of Congress, Ambassador Holbrooke, Excellencies, friends: Fifty-four years ago to the day, a young Jewish boy from a small town in the Carpathian Mountains woke up, not far from Goethe's beloved Weimar, in a place of eternal infamy called Buchenwald. He was finally free, but there was no joy in his heart. He thought there never would be again.

Liberated a day earlier by American soldiers, he remembers their rage at what they saw. And even if he lives to be a very old man, he will always be grateful to them for that rage, and also for their compassion. Though he did not understand their language, their eyes told him what he needed to know—that they, too, would remember, and bear witness.

And now, I stand before you, Mr. President—Commander-in-Chief of the army that freed me, and tens of thousands of others—and I am filled with a profound and abiding gratitude to the American people.

Gratitude is a word that I cherish. Gratitude is what defines the humanity of the human being. And I am grateful to you, Hillary—or Mrs. Clinton—for what you said, and for what you are doing for children in the world, for the homeless, for the victims of injustice, the victims of destiny and society. And I thank all of you for being here.

We are on the threshold of a new century, a new millennium. What will the legacy of this vanishing century be? How will it be remembered in the new millennium? Surely it will be judged, and judged severely, in both moral and metaphysical terms. These failures have cast a dark shadow over humanity: two

World Wars, countless civil wars, the senseless chain of assassinations—Gandhi, the Kennedys, Martin Luther King, Sadat, Rabin—bloodbaths in Cambodia and Nigeria, India and Pakistan, Ireland and Rwanda, Eritrea and Ethiopia, Sarajevo and Kosovo; the inhumanity in the gulag and the tragedy of Hiroshima. And, on a different level, of course, Auschwitz and Treblinka. So much violence, so much indifference.

What is indifference? Etymologically, the word means "no difference." A strange and unnatural state in which the lines blur between light and darkness, dusk and dawn, crime and punishment, cruelty and compassion, good and evil.

What are its courses and inescapable consequences? Is it a philosophy? Is there a philosophy of indifference conceivable?

ence reduces the other to an abstraction.

Over there, behind the black gates of Auschwitz, the most tragic of all prisoners were the "Muselmanner," as they were called. Wrapped in their torn blankets, they would sit or lie on the ground, staring vacantly into space, unaware of who or where they were, strangers to their surroundings. They no longer felt pain, hunger, thirst. They feared nothing. They felt nothing. They were dead and did not know it.

Rooted in our tradition, some of us felt that to be abandoned by humanity then was not the ultimate. We felt that to be abandoned by God was worse than to be punished by Him. Better an unjust God than an indifferent one. For us to be ignored by God was a harsher punishment than to be a victim of His anger.

"Indifference can be tempting—more than that, seductive.
It is so much easier to look away from victims.
It is so much easier to avoid such rude interruptions to our work,
our dreams, our hopes. It is, after all, awkward, troublesome,
to be involved in another person's pain and despair."

Can one possibly view indifference as a virtue? Is it necessary at times to practice it simply to keep one's sanity, live normally, enjoy a fine meal and a glass of wine, as the world around us experiences harrowing upheavals?

Of course, indifference can be tempting—more than that, seductive. It is so much easier to look away from victims. It is so much easier to avoid such rude interruptions to our work, our dreams, our hopes. It is, after all, awkward, troublesome, to be involved in another person's pain and despair. Yet, for the person who is indifferent, his or her neighbor are of no consequence. And, therefore, their lives are meaningless. Their hidden or even visible anguish is of no interest. Indiffer-

Man can live far from God—not outside God. God is wherever we are. Even in suffering? Even in suffering.

In a way, to be indifferent to that suffering is what makes the human being inhuman. Indifference, after all, is more dangerous than anger and hatred. Anger can at times be creative. One writes a great poem, a great symphony, one does something special for the sake of humanity because one is angry at the injustice that one witnesses. But indifference is never creative. Even hatred at times may elicit a response. You fight it. You denounce it. You disarm it. Indifference elicits no response. Indifference is not a response.

Indifference is not a beginning, it is an end. And, therefore, indifference is always the friend of the enemy,

for it benefits the aggressor—never his victim, whose pain is magnified when he or she feels forgotten. The political prisoner in his cell, the hungry children, the homeless refugees—not to respond to their plight, not to relieve their solitude by offering them a spark of hope is to exile them from human memory. And in denying their humanity we betray our own.

Indifference, then, is not only a sin, it is a punishment. And this is one of the most important lessons of this outgoing century's wide-ranging experiments in good and evil.

In the place that I come from, society was composed of three simple categories: the killers, the victims and the bystanders. During the darkest of times, inside the ghettos and death camps—and I'm glad that Mrs.

tion. They would have bombed the railways leading to Birkenau, just the railways, just once.

And now we knew, we learned, we discovered that the Pentagon knew, the State Department knew. And the illustrious occupant of the White House then, who was a great leader—and I say it with some anguish and pain, because today is exactly 54 years marking his death—Franklin Delano Roosevelt died on April 12, 1945, so he is very much present to me and to us.

No doubt, he was a great leader. He mobilized the American people and the world, going into battle, bringing hundreds and thousands of valiant and brave soldiers in America to fight fascism, to fight dictatorship, to fight Hitler. And so many of the young people fell in battle. And, nevertheless, his

"Indifference, after all, is more dangerous than anger and hatred. Anger can at times be creative. One writes a great poem, a great symphony, one does something special for the sake of humanity because one is angry at the injustice that one witnesses. But indifference is never creative."

Clinton mentioned that we are now commemorating that event, that period, that we are now in the Days of Remembrance—but then, we felt abandoned, forgotten. All of us did.

And our only miserable consolation was that we believed that Auschwitz and Treblinka were closely guarded secrets; that the leaders of the free world did not know what was going on behind those black gates and barbed wire; that they had no knowledge of the war against the Jews that Hitler's armies and their accomplices waged as part of the war against the Allies.

If they knew, we thought, surely those leaders would have moved heaven and earth to intervene. They would have spoken out with great outrage and convic-

image in Jewish history—I must say it—his image in Jewish history is flawed.

The depressing tale of the St. Louis is a case in point. Sixty years ago, its human cargo—maybe 1,000 Jews— was turned back to Nazi Germany. And that happened after the Kristallnacht, after the first state-sponsored pogrom, with hundreds of Jewish shops destroyed, synagogues burned, thousands of people put in concentration camps. And that ship, which was already on the shores of the United States, was sent back.

I don't understand. Roosevelt was a good man, with a heart. He understood those who needed help. Why didn't he allow these refugees to disembark? A thousand people—in America, a great country, the great-

est democracy, the most generous of all new nations in modern history. What happened? I don't understand. Why the indifference, on the highest level, to the suffering of the victims?

But then, there were human beings who were sensitive to our tragedy. Those non-Jews, those Christians, that we called the "Righteous Gentiles," whose selfless acts of heroism saved the honor of their faith. Why were they so few? Why was there a greater effort to save SS murderers after the war than to save their victims during the war?

Why did some of America's largest corporations continue to do business with Hitler's Germany until 1942? It has been suggested, and it was documented, that the Wehrmacht could not have conducted its in-

ed by a man who I believe that because of his crimes, should be charged with crimes against humanity. But this time, the world was not silent. This time, we do respond. This time, we intervene.

Does it mean that we have learned from the past? Does it mean that society has changed? Has the human being become less indifferent and more human? Have we really learned from our experiences? Are we less insensitive to the plight of victims of ethnic cleansing and other forms of injustices in places near and far? Is today's justified intervention in Kosovo, led by you, Mr. President, a lasting warning that never again will the deportation, the terrorization of children and their parents be allowed anywhere in the world? Will it discourage other dictators in other lands to do the same?

"Why did some of America's largest corporations continue to do business with Hitler's Germany until 1942? It has been suggested, and it was documented, that the Wehrmacht could not have conducted its invasion of France without oil obtained from American sources. How is one to explain their indifference?"

vasion of France without oil obtained from American sources. How is one to explain their indifference?

And yet, my friends, good things have also happened in this traumatic century: the defeat of Nazism, the collapse of communism, the rebirth of Israel on its ancestral soil, the demise of apartheid, Israel's peace treaty with Egypt, the peace accord in Ireland. And let us remember the meeting, filled with drama and emotion, between Rabin and Arafat that you, Mr. President, convened in this very place. I was here and I will never forget it.

And then, of course, the joint decision of the United States and NATO to intervene in Kosovo and save those victims, those refugees, those who were uproot-

What about the children? Oh, we see them on television, we read about them in the papers, and we do so with a broken heart. Their fate is always the most tragic, inevitably. When adults wage war, children perish. We see their faces, their eyes. Do we hear their pleas? Do we feel their pain, their agony? Every minute one of them dies of disease, violence, famine. Some of them—so many of them—could be saved.

And so, once again, I think of the young Jewish boy from the Carpathian Mountains. He has accompanied the old man I have become throughout these years of quest and struggle. And together we walk towards the new millennium, carried by profound fear and extraordinary hope.

60th Anniversary of the Liberation of Nazi Death Camps

SPEECH | UNITED NATIONS SPECIAL SESSION | JANUARY 24, 2005

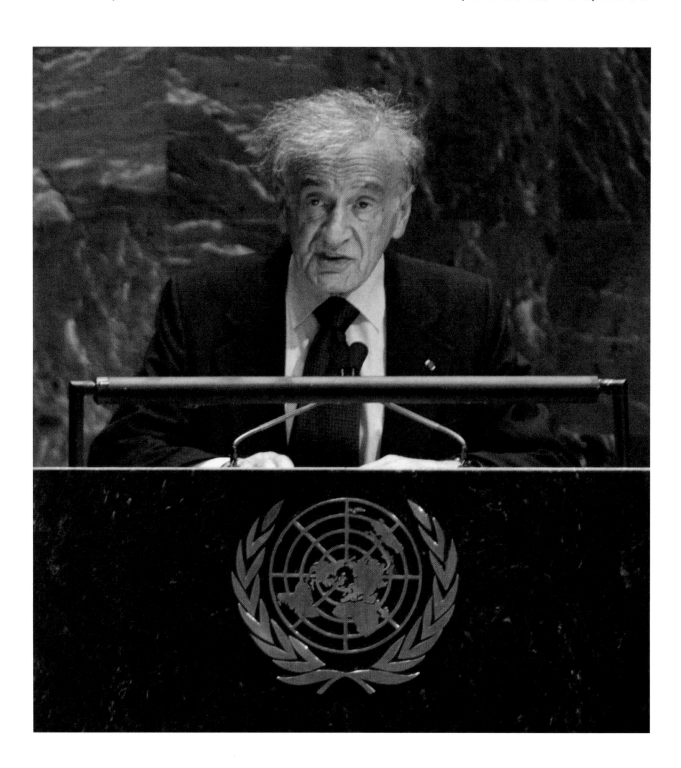

Mr. President of the General Assembly, Mr. Secretary-General my friend, excellencies:

The man who stands before you this morning feels deeply privileged. A teacher and writer, he speaks and writes as a witness to a crime committed in the heart of European Christendom and civilization by a brutal dictatorial regime—a crime of unprecedented cruelty in which all segments of government participated

When speaking about that era of darkness, the witness encounters difficulties. His words become obstacles rather than vehicles; he writes not with words but against words. For there are no words to describe what the victims felt when death was the norm and life a miracle. Still, whether you know it or not, his memory is part of yours.

positions in Germany. In recent years, that nation has become a true democracy. But the question remains open: In those dark years, what motivated so many brilliant and committed public servants to invent such horrors? By its scope and magnitude, by its sheer weight of numbers, by the impact of so much humiliation and pain, in spite of being the most documented tragedy in the annals of history, Auschwitz still defies language and understanding.

Let me evoke those times:

Babies used as target practice by SS men ...Adolescents condemned never to grow old ...Parents watching their children thrown into burning pits ...Immense solitude engulfing an entire people ...Infinite despair haunting our days and our dreams even 60 years later...

"It is not too late for today's children, ours and yours. It is for their sake alone that we bear witness. It is for their sake that we are duty-bound to denounce anti-Semitism, racism, and religious or ethnic hatred. Those who today preach and practice the cult of death, those who use suicide terrorism, the scourge of this new century, must be tried and condemned for crimes against humanity."

I speak to you as a son of an ancient people, the only people of antiquity to have survived antiquity, the Jewish people which, throughout much of its history, has endured exile and oppression yet has never given up hope of redemption

As a young adolescent, he saw what no human being should have to see: the triumph of political fanaticism and ideological hatred for those who were different. He saw multitudes of human beings humiliated, isolated, tormented, tortured and murdered. They were overwhelmingly Jews but there were others. And those who committed these crimes were not vulgar underworld thugs but men with high government, academic, industrial and medical

When did what we so poorly call the Holocaust begin? In 1938, during Kristallnacht? In 1939 perhaps, when a German ship, the St. Louis, with more than a thousand German Jewish refugees aboard, was turned back from America's shores? Or was it when the first massacres occurred in Babi Yar?

We still ask: What was Auschwitz: an end or a beginning, an apocalyptic consequence of centuries-old bigotry and hatred, or was it the final convulsion of demonic forces in human nature?

A creation parallel to God's—a world with its own antinomian United Nations of people of different nationalities, traditions, cultures, socioeconomic spheres, speaking many languages, clinging to a

variety of faiths and memories. They were grown-ups or young, but inside that world there were no children and no grandparents; they had already perished.

As I have said many times: Not all victims were Jewish, but all Jews were victims. For the first time in recorded history to be Jewish became a crime. Their birth became their death sentence. Correction: Jewish children were condemned to die even before they were born. What the enemy sought to attain was to put an end to Jewish history; what he wanted was a new world implacably, irrevocably devoid of Jews. Hence Auschwitz, Ponar, Treblinka, Belzec, Chelmno and Sobibor: dark factories of death erected for the Final Solution. Killers came there to kill and victims to die.

That was Auschwitz, an executioner's ideal of a kingdom of absolute evil and malediction with its princes and beggars, philosophers and theologians, politicians and artists, a place where to lose a piece of bread meant losing life, and a smile from a friend another day of promise.

At the time, the witness tried to understand; he still does not: How was such calculated evil, such bottomless and pointless cruelty possible? Had Creation gone mad? Had God covered His face? A religious person cannot conceive of Auschwitz either with or without God. But what about man? How could intelligent, educated or simple law-abiding citizens fire machine guns at hundreds of children and their parents, and in the evening enjoy a cadence by Schiller, a partita by Bach?

Turning point or watershed, that tremendous catastrophe which has traumatized history has forever changed man's perception of responsibility toward other human beings. The sad, terrible fact is that had the Western nations intervened when Hitler occupied Czechoslovakia and Austria; had America accepted more refugees from Europe; had Britain allowed more Jews to return to their ancestral land; had the Allies bombed the railways leading to Birkenau, our tragedy might have been avoided, its scope surely diminished.

This shameful indifference we must remember, just as we must remember to thank the few heroic individuals who, like Raoul Wallenberg, risked their lives to save Jews. We shall also always remember the armies that liberated Europe and the soldiers who liberated the death-camps, the Americans in Buchenwald, the Russians in Auschwitz and the British in Belsen. But for many victims they all came too late. That we must also remember.

When the American Third Army liberated Buchenwald, there was no joy in our heart: only pain. We did not sing, we did not celebrate. We had just enough strength to recite the Kaddish.

And now, 60 years later, you who represent the entire world community, listen to the words of the witness. Like Jeremiah and Job, we could have cried and cursed the days dominated by injustice and violence. We could have chosen vengeance. We did not. We could have chosen hate. We did not. Hatred is degrading and vengeance demeaning. They are diseases. Their history is dominated by death.

The Jewish witness speaks of his people's suffering as a warning. He sounds the alarm so as to prevent these things being done. He knows that for the dead it is too late; for them, abandoned by God and betrayed by humanity, victory came much too late.

But it is not too late for today's children, ours and yours. It is for their sake alone that we bear witness. It is for their sake that we are duty-bound to denounce anti-Semitism, racism and religious or ethnic hatred. Those who today preach and practice the cult of death, those who use suicide terrorism, the scourge of this new century, must be tried and condemned for crimes against humanity. Suffering confers no privileges; it is what one does with suffering that matters. Yes, the past is in the present, but the future is still in our hands.

Those who survived Auschwitz advocate hope, not despair; generosity, not rancor or bitterness; gratitude, not violence. We must be engaged, we must reject indifference as an option. Indifference always helps the aggressor, never his victims. And what is memory if not a noble and necessary response to and against indifference?

But...will the world ever learn?

Inauguration of the Holocaust History Museum

SPEECH | YAD VASHEM, JERUSALEM | MARCH 15, 2005

Mr. President, Mr. Prime Minister, *Mes Amis de France*, *Nitsolei Shoa Yekarim*:

As you walk through the museum, so magnificently conceived by Moshe Safdie, you wonder: Where is the place of rage in all that? How come that the Jewish people, when we discovered the magnitude of cruelty and the consequences of hatred, how come that we were not possessed by an extraordinary, implacable rage—rage of the killers; rage toward those who inspired the killers; rage toward the indifferent—those who knew and were silent? Where is rage?

So you look and you look, and you are afraid to look. I am. I look at some pictures of Jews from Hungary and I am afraid to discover some that I have known. You read and you read, and you say to yourself: Where did they have the strength to write, to use words, destined to whom?

My good friends, all of us know more or less that there was a tragedy; and we also know we must be honest about it: There are no words.

Only those who were there know what it meant being there. And yet, we are duty-bound to try and not

to bury our memories into silence. We try. I know what people say: "It's so easy." Those that were there won't agree with that statement. The statement is: "It was man's inhumanity to man." No! It was man's inhumanity to Jews. Jews were not killed because they were human beings. In the eyes of the killers, they were not human beings! They were Jews! It is because they were Jews that it was so easy for the killers to kill!

And you see the pictures. My god, you see the pictures. Jews were ordered to dig their own graves. Have we ever had that in history, which always is filled with cruelty—but not such cruelty? Have mothers ever been forced to give up their children in order to live? And few mothers chose that, no? Mothers went with their children, with their babies—there are no words.

martyrs. In those times the heroes were martyrs and the martyrs were heroes. It was heroic for a friend to give his piece of bread to his friend. It was heroic to go around on Shabbat and simply say to his or her friends: "It's Shabbat, today." It was heroic to have faith; it was heroic to be human.

And so we go through the museum and what should we do? Weep? No. My good friends, we never try to tell the tale to make people weep. It's too easy. We didn't want pity. If we decided to tell the tale, it is because we wanted the world to be a better world—just a better world, and learn, and remember.

There is a frightening character in all of Kafka's stories. It's always the messenger who tried to deliver the message and is unable to do so. We feel sorry for a poor

"Jews were ordered to dig their own graves. Have we ever had that in history, which always is filled with cruelty—but not such cruelty? Have mothers ever been forced to give up their children in order to live? And few mothers chose that, no? Mothers went with their children, with their babies—there are no words."

At that time we had a feeling that history had entered into madness, and madness had its own logic, its own destiny, almost its own archeology. And within that madness it was perfectly plausible to kill children.

And so, we go through the museum and we don't understand. All we know is that it happened. And now the question is: What does one do with memories?

Any psychiatrist will tell you, if you suppress memories they come back with fury. You must face them. Even if you cannot articulate them, we must face them. And memories are many and varied: memories of those who died with weapons in their hands; and those who died with prayers on their lips. And let no one say that some were heroes and others

messenger. But there is something more tragic than that: when the messenger has delivered the message and nothing has changed.

You heard tonight those who spoke here with elegance, with compassion, and they spoke already about anti-Semitism and intolerance. Now? Sixty years later? When the messenger has tried to deliver the message? Why should there be anti-Semitism? But there is. Why should there be suicide killers? But there are. Why should there be hatred? But there is. Fanaticism? Yes! It's calmed? No, it's here!

The messenger has delivered the message. What is our role?

We must become the messengers' messengers.

"Heart to Heart"

INTERVIEW | MOMENT MAGAZINE | MAY/JUNE 2013

In 2011, Elie underwent emergency open-heart surgery, and in the following year, even the walk from his desk to the couch seemed to tire him and his already soft voice was quieter than ever. But when I visited him in Florida during the winter of 2013, I was delighted to see that he once again exuded energy, and his eyes had regained their slightly mischievous twinkle. We discussed what he described as his "third brush with death" (preceded by the Holocaust and being struck by a taxi in Times Square), which he wrote about in his final book, *Open Heart*. (The selfies above were taken in his office in New York City in 2015.)—*Nadine Epstein*

As you describe in *Open Heart*, you recently had open-heart surgery. Was facing death in the hospital different from facing death in Auschwitz? There I wasn't alone. I was with my father, as long as he was alive. I was always with others. Nobody was alone, yet everyone was lonelier than ever before. So it's not the same thing. Here, I was alone in this condition. I knew I could die. I had, of course, as I say, lived in death over there. But here, it was an "I"—not "us."

Can we ever prepare for death? There comes a moment when you feel maybe this is the last time that I think the way I do, the last time I see people, the last time I will see my son or my wife. And therefore, you have to prepare yourself.

Even after the war, a few months after I came to New York, a taxi ran over me in Times Square, and it was a

the living more than to the dead. Whatever is living is pure; whatever is not living is impure. The laws of mourning in Judaism are so marvelous. Our sages have invested so much in those laws. As long as the person is alive, everything is centered on him or her. Everything. You may do anything to save that person's life. Then after death, the interest of the sages is directed to the survivors: What does one do when he or she loses a mother or father?

In *Night,* you write, "Never shall I forget those moments that murdered my God and my soul and turned my dreams to ashes." Has your approach to God changed since, and did you think about God in the hospital? What I wrote in *Night* is a protest and a question, and I stand by every word I wrote. It's an outcry, an agonizing outcry. I come from a very

"There comes a moment when you feel maybe this is the last time that I think the way I do, the last time I see people, the last time I will see my son or my wife. And therefore, you have to prepare yourself."

miracle that I survived. That said, the Jew must prepare himself because death could happen that day. Every morning when we get up is a prayer of gratitude. Thank God for being awake, for having survived my sleep. The fact is, to die is something we all have in common. We still are looking for someone who knows the secret of immortality. Only God is immortal; we are not. The Hasidic masters prepare themselves everyday: What if I die tomorrow? What if this is my last prayer? With what am I going to present myself to God before the celestial tribunal where I shall appear afterwards?

How does Judaism teach us to confront death? One of the most important mitzvot in the Torah is, "And you shall choose life." It also means that you should choose the living and that you must be faithful to

religious background. I spoke to God, against God, but the next day, somebody managed to smuggle in a pair of tefillin, portions of bread, and together with my father we got up early and stood in line just to say the morning prayers. My disappointment was with man—what should I expect of man, both good and bad. But with God, the question, "Where is God?" has obsessed me for many years and still does without an answer. Even in the hospital, I couldn't not think about that question. Without faith there is no question. I remain profoundly attached, of course, to my parents and grandparents. I said, "What good do I do to them if I say goodbye to God?" But I didn't, because what good would it do to them? It's really because of my grandfather and my father that I say to God, I pray to you and I bless your name.

Which language did you think in as you conversed with death in the hospital? In Yiddish. It was, after all, my first language. The language I think in depends on the topic and the period. If it's about my childhood, I think in Yiddish, because that was my language. If it's about America, I think in English, but if it's about literature or philosophy, it goes back to French.

Do you feel that your life work of teaching about the Holocaust has made a difference? I was invited two or three years ago to address the General Assembly of the United Nations, and I chose the topic, "Will the world learn?" I came out with the answer, no. It will not learn, because it has not learned. Otherwise, how else would one explain Cambodia and

God, because what else do I have? My disbelief cannot stop them. I disbelieve in many certainties, but then I said okay, there are children in the world, and there I should say, no, no, I need to have faith for their sake.

That brings me to one of the most moving passages in *Open Heart*. You tell the story of your grandson Elijah's visit to you after your surgery when you were in great pain. This is one of the most beautiful stories of my life. He came and sat on my bed, and said, "Grandpa, I know you suffered a lot, and you have great pain. But you know how much I love you, tell me, if I loved you more, would you suffer less?" The words of the philosophers were on his lips.

"He came and sat on my bed, and said, 'Grandpa, I know you suffered a lot, and you have great pain. But you know how much I love you, tell me, if I loved you more, would you suffer less?' The words of the philosophers were on his lips."

genocide, and the hunger and humiliation—how else would you explain it? We haven't learned. And maybe it's our fault—mine and my colleagues— maybe we haven't done enough. And yet we've tried.

If Auschwitz can't convince man to end violence, what can? That's what I said, if Auschwitz didn't cure the disease, what can? But still we must try. When the last survivor will be gone—my God, I don't want to be that one. When the last will be gone, a page will be turned. That's what I say wherever I go, I say to young people to be a witness is to become one, because now you are our witnesses.

Do you still believe in humanity? I believe in humanity against humanity, I believe in God against

What did you say to him? Of course, absolutely. I wanted him to love me more.

Did your open-heart surgery make you a stronger person? I don't know, I'd say more knowledgeable. I know more about my own limitations. I realize that to our great embarrassment, there are great moments in life with such pain that a pill has more weight than all the books by Kant, Schopenhauer and Nietzsche. Just a pill, more important than all these great books written by great men and women since history began. It makes you very humble. We are vulnerable, and therefore humble.

Is there anything else you'd like to do with your life? To begin again.

About Night

Reflections from Young Readers & Discussion Questions

Reflections on *Night*

In 2016, *Moment* asked young readers to tell us how *Night* influenced their lives.

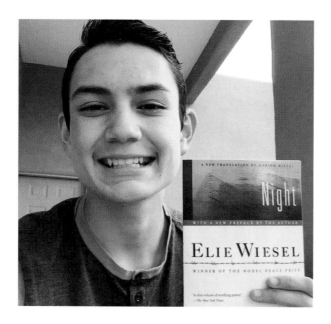

Adan Armijo

Albuquerque, New Mexico

Meredith Caine

Alexandria, Virginia

If you aren't aware of what has happened in the world, how is it possible to improve your future? To me this question has a very simple answer: You cannot. You cannot learn this lesson any better than through reading *Night*. Reading Elie Wiesel's book opened my eyes and gave me the ability to look beyond propaganda to realize what is going on in the world today. His writing influenced my goal in life. I want to be a lawyer so I can help those in need who are being discriminated against for circumstances not under their control. *Night* gave me the courage to want to become something more than myself.

As a non-Jew, it is impossible for me to understand the Holocaust or the experiences of those who fell victim to it. However, *Night* gave me the chance to read about it, to be told, "This is what happened. It was horrible. It was real. It happened to me and to so many others." Even though I cannot understand the Holocaust, knowing that it happened and knowing what so many innocent human beings went through, is important. I will never forget Wiesel's story. I will never forget how he and the Jewish people were treated. I will never forget the Nazis. They won't get their final victory of erasure because Elie Wiesel refused to be silent.

Jesse Edelstein

Ann Arbor, Michigan

I grew up hearing the stories of my grandparents, who both survived the Holocaust, but when I read *Night*, it was in a different setting than I was used to: The text was assigned for my 9th-grade English class. I was able to see the impact that *Night* had on a group of teenagers who had had little exposure to the harsh realities of the Holocaust. It was amazing to see how well Elie Wiesel was able to speak to this group of young people. *Night* is such a powerful memoir because it reaches out to people of all ages, races and religions. It will keep the memories of the Holocaust alive for future generations, even when Elie Wiesel and other survivors aren't physically present to recall their stories.

Noam Ginsburg

Los Angeles, California

I am Jewish, and I am and always have been proud of it. Still, I never felt as strong a connection to my people as I did when I read Elie Wiesel's story. Every second I spent in the eyes of Eliezer, the more I felt connected to what was happening. I was there with him as the SS officers whipped him in the middle of the room, with people watching, and in the moment when he felt like the corpses that lay in front of him. After reading a portion of the book one morning, I thought of how I would react if the Nazis, or any other group, were to invade my town, my country, and the idea was terrifying. I have loved books my whole life, but this is the first book that I will go on to read at least 10 more times. I have been brought so much closer to my people. From now on, when a fellow Jew cries or laughs, I will cry and laugh with them. Now I know more about the pain they feel, the pain I now feel as well.

Ashley Hammett
Bowie, Maryland

Elie Wiesel lived through the ghettos, concentration camps and deplorable treatment that millions of other Jews experienced as the Holocaust. But through his turmoil, he gained a voice. He spoke for those who never got the chance to. The authentic emotion conveyed by Elie's words gave me a look into the pain of millions. When Elie's father thinks he will be selected by the SS to be executed, he gives Elie a spoon. He thinks that he will no longer need to eat because he will be dead. This item is the only inheritance that his father has left him, adding to the emotion of the scene. The suspense builds as a bereaved Elie describes how he goes through his day thinking that his father has been killed, and the tension is released when we learn that there was a second selection and his father was spared. This book is an amazing and insightful look into the Holocaust.

Shira Minsk
Rockville, Maryland

The first few pages of *Night* reveal a lesson. As ignorance prevailed in Sighet with regard to the war around them, the townspeople believed themselves to be safe. They shut their ears to Moishe the Beadle's experiences, turned a blind eye to the events foreshadowed by the restrictions on the Jews of Sighet and ruled out escaping to Palestine and other places because it was too inconvenient. Although optimism and hope are invaluable weapons in combating peril and distress, to me Elie's reflections are a call to not lose sight of reality or confuse hope with a false sense of safety.

Night is a humble request not only to never forget the tragedies of the Holocaust, as we so often say, but to never again become complacent, to never again lose sight of reality, and to never again allow ourselves and others to be hurt by things that we could have prevented, on a scale small or large.

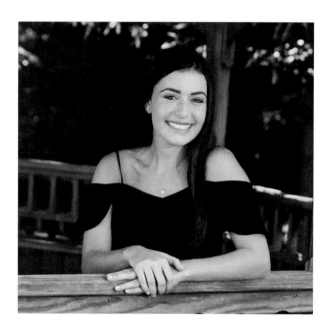

Carol Silber

Washington, DC

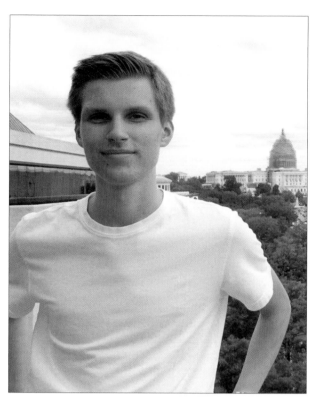

N*ight* tells a story of total destruction. This past spring, I had the privilege of visiting Poland and Prague with my classmates. We, too, witnessed total destruction. We stood in beautiful synagogues in Prague that were once staples of vibrant Jewish communities but today are simply tourist attractions. We gathered in a small room in Theresienstadt, where words of Jewish prayer are fading from the walls. And we saw places of destruction, too—Plaszow, Auschwitz-Birkenau and Majdanek.

But our trip did not end with total destruction. We spent one of our last days in Europe at the JCC in Krakow with Rabbi Avi Baumol, who seeks out the children and grandchildren of Jews who stayed in Europe after the Holocaust but hid their religious identity, and offers to introduce them to Judaism.

While *Night* ends with total destruction, Elie Wiesel's life did not. He went on to advocate against human evil, to speak out against genocide and injustice, to constantly strive for a better tomorrow. With him gone, my generation and the ones that come after it must find ways to continue this pursuit—at home, in Israel and in seemingly unlikely places, like a JCC in Krakow.

Thomas Siurkus

Stuttgart, Germany

I n Germany, we don't usually read personal Holocaust testimonies in school; we learn about the topic in a more academic way, through facts and statistics. *Night* is very different from the accounts of other Holocaust survivors. While other survivors whose stories I read mainly listed what happened to them, Elie Wiesel created a great literary work. The metaphor of *Night* is awesome; it is a page-turner. Reading it helped me understand the human dimension of the Holocaust.

It is important to read the personal story of a single survivor. If we don't talk about individuals, then this becomes Hitler's victory. Hitler wanted us to only think about numbers and not about human beings. Reading this book inspired me to learn about the Holocaust, and it taught me that you must never be silent. We have to speak up for those who can't speak for themselves; that's one of the most important lessons of the Holocaust.

Elior Waskow

Washington, DC

Matthew Wieseltier

Washington, DC

I've read *Night* four different times, and each time I get something new out of the book. Each reading has led to a more complete understanding of the horrific events of the Holocaust. *Night*, however, is much more than just a recounting of the evil of the Nazis.

The story begins when Elie Wiesel is 15 years old, roughly the same age as I am now. I couldn't help but compare his life to mine. As a victim of the Holocaust, most of his teenage years were taken away. Around the time in his life that Wiesel was deported, along with his family, to Auschwitz, I was preparing to finish ninth grade. Despite these differences, there are some surprising similarities illustrated in his memoir. Like me, Wiesel grew up going to synagogue every week and was just a normal teenager hanging out with his sisters and going to school.

Wiesel struggled with many of the same things that I do. He questions his belief in God, religion and community; questions that are just as relevant today. This is one reason that the memoir transcends time and remains one of the most critically acclaimed and brilliant pieces of literature written on the Holocaust.

Night is emotionally wrenching. It intertwines faith, family and history so that each theme is explored to its fullest potential, while also not crowding each other out. There are a couple of chapters in the book solely dedicated to each theme. In one of the chapters on faith, one can tell how much thought Mr. Wiesel put into writing it and how much conflict and pain he endured. While telling the reader many of the terrible things that happened to him in the concentration camps, Mr. Wiesel also adds emotion, which gives the book a certain realism that isn't found in documents that were written solely for historic purposes.

To read *Night* is an extremely important thing to do as a Jew and as a citizen of the world. As a Jew and a grandson of Holocaust survivors, I had always known that this catastrophe happened, but I had never explored the emotions and the horrors that went on during it because I was too young. After reading *Night*, however, I felt as if my Jewish and moral education had been furthered considerably because it is such a profound book.

It's up to you now,
and we shall help you—
we must ensure that my past
does not become your future.

ELIE WIESEL

UN WORLD PEACE DAY,
SEPTEMBER 21, 2006
NEW YORK CITY

Photo: Elie and Elisha Wiesel in New York after it was announced that Elie won the 1986 Nobel Peace Prize.

Discussion Questions

These questions are designed for classrooms and study groups.

1) What scenes from *Night* do you remember most vividly? Did reading the book change the way you look at the world, political leaders or your friends and family?

2) In his 1986 Nobel Peace Prize acceptance speech, Elie Wiesel said: "One person of integrity can make a difference, a difference of life and death. As long as one dissident is in prison, our freedom will not be true. As long as one child is hungry, our life will be filled with anguish and shame. What all these victims need above all is to know that they are not alone; that we are not forgetting them, that when their voices are stifled we shall lend them ours, that while their freedom depends on ours, the quality of our freedom depends on theirs." In what ways did the actions of Elie Wiesel's life reflect the meaning of these words? How does this quote relate to your own role in the world around you?

3) In *Night* Eliezer describes his life before and during the Holocaust. How is his life similar to yours? How is it different?

4) Who did you identify with most in *Night*? Who did you most admire in the book?

5) There are people today who insist that the Holocaust never happened and that it was really only a minor event that has been greatly exaggerated. How do you think Elie Wiesel would respond to those people?

6) Some parents have protested that they do not want their children to read *Night* because it is so grim. How would you respond to those who say that the book should not be required reading in public schools?

7) Elie Wiesel believed that the most dangerous and destructive thing for mankind was not hatred but indifference. What do you think he meant by this? Do you agree with him?

8) Why do you think Elie Wiesel wrote *Night*?

Photo: Elie and fellow Nobel Peace Prize-winner Lech Walesa at the former Auschwitz-Birkenau death camp in Poland in January, 1988.

9) In his 1986 Nobel lecture, Elie Wiesel spoke of the power of memory, including the idea that the memory of death can serve as a shield against death. He mentions several sources of injustice in the 1980s such as Apartheid in South Africa, as well as fears that are still with us, such as terrorism and the threat of nuclear war. Do you think the 21st century will be distinguished by remembrance, or by forgetting?

10) In *Night* Eliezer expresses sympathy for Job, the biblical figure who experienced tremendous losses as Satan and God debated Job's faithfulness. After watching the lynching and slow death of a young boy, Eliezer believes that God is hanging from the gallows as well. In his 1986 Nobel lecture, Elie Wiesel describes the Holocaust as "a universe where God, betrayed by His creatures, covered His face in order not to see." How did Wiesel's relationship with God evolve and change over the course of his life? In general, how do you think survivors of the Holocaust reconciled their experiences with their faith?

11) In the final pages of *Night*, Elie Wiesel describes his own face reflected in a mirror. He writes that a corpse stared back at him with a look that has never left him. What aspects of Elie Wiesel died during the ordeal of the Holocaust? Which parts of him were born in their place? What do you make of his observation that among the men liberated with him, none of them ever sought revenge?

12) *Night* was initially rejected by numerous major publishing houses in both the United States and France. *Night* is now a classic that has inspired numerous other works. What is unique about Elie Wiesel's story? How does his approach compare with the work of other memoirists who you have read?

13) Could an event like the Holocaust happen today? Could it happen in the United States? Who would be the potential victims? How would you respond if an event like the Holocaust occurred today?

14) What have you learned about Elie Wiesel from this book that you didn't know before? How has that affected you?

Afterword

BY TED KOPPEL

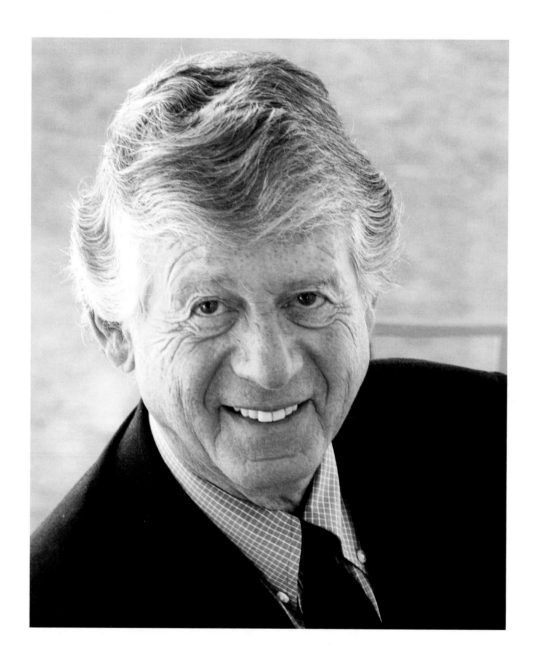

Ted Koppel was the anchor for ABC's Nightline from 1980 to 2005.
He is currently a contributor to CBS News Sunday Morning.

"Elie performed the alchemy of converting pain, injustice and horror into love, compassion and tolerance."

As Will Rogers, the Oklahoma cowboy, once noted: "We're all ignorant; just about different things." Before my old friend Elie slips, irretrievably, into secular sainthood, let me offer a couple of affectionate remembrances that underscore the point.

When it came to popular American culture, for example, Elie was clueless. Over a succession of many winters, Elie taught at Eckerd College in St. Petersburg, Florida. Just across the bay from Tampa, the two cities are frequently conjoined, Tampa-St. Pete, as though they were a single entity. One could not, in mid-winter of 2009, live in the bay area and avoid the news that Tampa was about to host the Pittsburgh Steelers and the Arizona Cardinals for what has been, in recent years, the most watched television event of every year—the Super Bowl. Somewhere in the neighborhood of one hundred million Americans annually watch the game. Need I add that Elie Wiesel was never among them? When I visited with Elie late that January, the region was aflutter with banners, plastered with posters announcing the game. It should not have been possible for anyone to be alive and sentient in the Tampa Bay area without experiencing the mounting fever. Elie remained unaware, not simply of that particular game, but of the existence of the Super Bowl itself.

On another occasion, I picked Elie up at Washington's National Airport in order to drive him to a gathering of *Nightline* staffers. *Nightline* was the television news program I hosted at that time and we were having a retreat. Elie had agreed to speak with the staff as a favor to me: ("If you ask me to do it, of course I'll be there." Few people faced more demands on their time, while more generously sharing it with their friends.) I had stopped at a gas station to refuel. When I got back in the car, Elie looked at me with beaming admiration: "You know how to do that," he said. "Do what?" I asked—genuinely confused. "Put gas in the car," said my friend, clearly in awe of a highly technical skill that he did not possess.

In January of 1996 Elie was invited to be a guest at President Clinton's State of the Union address. Whenever possible, on his visits to Washington, Elie would come to our home for conversation and coffee; and, earlier that day, he and I were talking about that evening's event. I noted that Elie would certainly be seated next to the First Lady. Elie dismissed the notion out of hand. There had, I reminded Elie, been some recent friction between the Clinton White House and the Jewish community. I teased Elie that he was about to become a political prop; that his highly visible presence next to Mrs. Clinton would be taken as a signal that the damage had been repaired. That was too cynical for Elie's taste: "I'll bet you," he said. We settled on the symbolic amount of a Susan B. Anthony silver dollar. It arrived in the mail a few days later.

In late December of 1999, Elie and Marion visited our family at a home we owned back then in Captiva, Florida. Another family was with us that New Year's Eve. All of the "children," theirs and ours, were fully grown adults, so we opted to take advantage of Elie's presence as the millennium ended for a serious and wide-ranging conversation. I proposed a hypothetical: "What if terrorists planted a bomb inside the World Trade Center? One of the terrorists is apprehended and you, Elie, are president. Thousands of lives are at stake. Time is of the essence. The prisoner knows where the bomb is located. Do you authorize torture?"

"President" Wiesel did not hesitate. "No," he said. "I cannot."

That same trip revealed another, more playful side of Elie. On the first day of the New Year, I convinced Elie that he needed to take up bicycling again. He hadn't been on a bike since his childhood, he claimed. I threw a couple of bikes in the back of our rental car and took Elie to a secluded spot. He made it just about 20 yards before he crashed the bike. He was wearing shorts, and one of his knees was bloodied. Our reaction? Laughter. We could both imagine the headlines: "Koppel injures Nobel Laureate." To the best of my knowledge, Elie never rode a bike again!

Elie's words earlier that New Year's Eve were, in retrospect, an eerie premonition of a real event that would test the moral fiber of an actual U.S. president less than two years later. We can only speculate on how differently the first two decades of

up a car, the Super Bowl. He was anything but an intellectual snob. He would have liked to know how to refuel a car; but absent the ability to drive, there had never been the occasion to learn. A life-long struggle against inhumanity had left little room for the ordinary, the mundane. He was willing to try, but had lost the knack.

It occurs to me that living with Elie, navigating him through the mysteries of ordinary life and around the pitfalls prepared by the cynical for the unwary must, at times, have been a heavy burden for Marion Wiesel. No one can ever doubt her love for Elie, but icons are, almost by definition, impractical creatures.

We remember Elie with a particular sense of loss precisely because he was unlike almost everyone else we know. He was an impractical man with unrealistic expectations. You will, I hope, have come

"We remember Elie with a particular sense of loss precisely because he was unlike almost everyone else we know."

the 21st century might have unfolded if events had been dictated by a man incapable of tolerating, let alone authorizing inhumanity.

Elie Wiesel would probably have been an ineffective president. He was, you know, offered the presidency of Israel at one point, but turned it down. Actually, that presidency, largely symbolic in nature, might have suited him well. But ours? He would have been incapable of the shallowness, the sheer nastiness. Elie Wiesel could never have adjusted to the constant demands of moral compromise. He was, simply, an unwavering symbol of uncompromising decency.

I have highlighted Elie's ethereal nature by deliberately stressing his unfamiliarity with what most of us would consider the ordinary: gassing

to know Elie a little better through some of the remembrances shared in these chapters. He performed the alchemy of converting pain, injustice and horror into love, compassion and tolerance. We remember him not so much because he so often succeeded but because he never stopped trying. He taught us that all acts of inhumanity are similar. Intolerance and hatred because of a person's race, religion or ethnicity are equally unacceptable. He didn't expect to win that argument but insisted that the principle be maintained. Elie echoed Micah—encouraging us to do justice, love mercy and walk humbly with our God. Trying was the thing; because the ultimate evil in Elie Wiesel's eyes, the reason his example should live on with us, is that we must never give in to indifference.